AN HONEST PUBLIC SERVANT

A Brief Biography Of

MANUEL LUJAN

Republican Congressman
Of New Mexico, 1968-1988
Secretary of Interior
Of the United States, 1989-1993

BY PAUL N. "PETE" McCLOSKEY, JR.

Member of Congress, 1967-1983

For information:
Pete McCloskey
P.O. Box 158
Cerrillos, New Mexico, 87010
email: rumseyfarm@aol.com

Published by:
Eaglet Books, P.O. Box 3, Rumsey, California 95679

Book Cover and Interior Design
by Barbara Fail, Studio 14 Productions, Madrid, NM
studio14madrid@gmail.com

ISBN 978-0-692-78779-3
Pete McCloskey

TABLE OF CONTENTS

FOREWORD

Not too long ago, at the advanced age of 88, a famous Pulitzer Prize winning author, A. B. Guthrie, Jr., started on a new book to match his great works, "The Big Sky" and "The Way West." Asked about it, he stated simply: "Even at 88 I think every man should have a project."

Guthrie died before the book could be finished.

On my reaching his age of 88, increasingly feeble, with failing eyesight, hearing, and memory, and looking for a project, I thought it might be worthwhile to write a brief biography about a friend, Manny Lujan, a rare individual I had come to highly respect. I would add a few words about the history of his home state and the times we served together in Congress, between 1968 and 1982, a bygone, nearly-forgotten era.

Manny Lujan Jr.'s story is an amazing one, and that of his parents, Manuel Sr. and Lorenzita Romero Lujan, is equally impressive. Manny Jr.'s life and growth as a public servant paralleled the same years that his native state of New Mexico was growing from a somewhat impoverished Hispanic/Indian community during the Great Depression years to become the center of research and labor by the world's greatest scientists. Its research laboratories at Los Alamos and Albuquerque, working with those at Berkeley and Livermore in California, have given the United States the most powerful military weapons in the world. Even now, the improvements on the atomic and even deadlier hydrogen bomb are being worked on daily only a few miles from the once quiet community of Santa Fe where Manny grew up.

There are many reasons why the story of Manny Lujan

Jr., his parents, and the Lujans who preceded him during the long history of New Mexico, should be preserved.

First, Manny is too humble a man to ever write or commission his own biography. Even now, he has no idea what an inspiration his life has been to the host of people who have known him. Further, it is doubtful that even the people of New Mexico know what an incredible and honest representative they had in Washington for 24 years.

Manny Lujan is that rarest of political animals; a quiet, generous, and completely honest man, not given to thunderous oratory, but one who entered politics more with a sense of public duty than one seeking power or glory. But there is steel and quiet pride behind his friendly visage, characteristics justifiably earned by the descendants of people who braved the harsh lands and climate of New Mexico for over 400 years.

Second, Manny is a direct descendant of the first Lujan to come to New Mexico, as a soldier and potential settler with the Oñate Expedition of 1598. That's nine years before the English landed at Jamestown in 1607, and 22 years before Pilgrims landed from the Mayflower at Plymouth Rock in 1620.

That first Lujan to arrive in New Mexico was a 27-year old native of the Canary Islands. The records show that he was accompanied by an Indian servant, with whom he is believed to have fathered at least one child. Three hundred and thirty years later, Manny was born in 1928 in San Ildefonso, not far from where Oñate established the first capital of New Mexico. Most of those 330 years were ones of great peril and privation, with continuing neglect and/or oppression from Mexico and the Catholic Church. The settlers, facing a harsh land and difficult climate for growing food, lived in constant fear of raids by the Apaches from the south and west, the Navajos and Utes from the north, and the Comanches from the east.

Manny knew his grandfather, Martin Lujan, a Hispanic homesteader, whose farm was located on the remote Pajarito Plateau above the San Ildefonso Indian Reservation. His father, Manny Sr., was also a farmer, whose property adjoined that of his grandfather. His father moved to Santa Fe in 1929, and Manny worked for him, first on his farm, and then in his insurance business in Santa Fe, obtaining a degree from St. Michael's College and starting his own insurance agency in Albuquerque. At the age of 40, he was elected to the United States Congress in a stunning upset of a popular Democratic incumbent, in a heavily Democrat District that covered most of Northern New Mexico, from Albuquerque north to the Colorado line, and to the borders of Oklahoma and Texas on the east.

Unlike most of the New Mexican politicians who preceded him, Manuel Lujan Jr., like his father, was a man of impeccable honesty. Retiring after 20 years in Congress, looking forward to going back home, he thought long and hard when offered the position of Secretary of the Interior by his friend, George H.W. Bush. But people don't turn down Presidents who ask for their assistance in the governance of our country. Manny served four years as the Trustee of America's finest parks, historic areas, and landscapes, without a taint of scandal or dishonesty. He quietly left Washington to return to New Mexico in 1993, and unlike the majority of his colleagues, he eschewed the offers of enormous compensation in lobbying and administrative positions in the nation's Capitol. New Mexico and its people were more important to him than the sense of power inside the Beltway.

Such a man, after 24 years of public service, deserves a biography.

Another reason for this book is to remind myself that once there was a much different Republican Party, one where we dealt with respect and courtesy with Democrats, men of opposite parties like Chuck Percy and Adlai Stevenson Jr. of Illinois, John Chafee and Claiborne Pell of New Jersey, Don Riegle and John Dingell of Michigan, Tip O'Neill and Syl Conte of Massachusetts, Mo Udall and Barry Goldwater of Arizona, all working to craft legislative compromises to address the great problems of their time, like Social Security and immigration. It has been fun to recall some of the events that brought Manny and me together in the years of Gerry Ford and George Bush the Elder. Manny pretty well exemplified the kinder, gentler ideal of our mutual friend, George H.W. Bush.

And too, there are a number of famous people who have shaped both of our lives, among them Katharine "Peach" Mayer of Santa Fe, the leading lady and grande dame of Republican politics from 1964 until her death in 1985. She and her husband, Walter, are worthy of a story in their own right. Her husband, Walter, was a partner in ranching and farming with Manuel Lujan Sr., and served as a mentor to Manny in his youth, tutoring him in the livestock business and irrigated farming.

Then, there was John Ehrlichman, my law school debate partner and friend, who controlled the 1972 Republican convention where Manny became famous for casting the sole vote that was perceived as the first vote against Nixon's terrible bombing, not just in Viet Nam, but in Laos and Cambodia as well. After serving 16 months at the Safford Federal Penitentiary for his part in the Watergate cover up,

Ehrlichman retired to Santa Fe and was befriended by Peach Mayer, that mortal enemy of the bombing which Nixon had conducted with Ehrlichman's approval.

As I have studied the stories of Manny's life, I have come to look upon his parents and the Mayers as key players in Manny's rise to greatness. Manny fully realizes this... that his parents, and Peach and Walter Mayer, gave him a great head start in bringing honesty to Republican politics in New Mexico. To be the first honest Republican Secretary of the Interior from New Mexico should be considered an honor of the highest magnitude. A Republican predecessor, Albert B. Fall, had served as Secretary of the Interior in the 1920s but was indicted and sent to jail for his part in the Infamous Teapot Dome scandal.

That Manny would cast the first Republican vote to end the bombing in Southeast Asia was a major event in his life and mine, but also an important milestone in our country's history. It was a significant event... the Congressional decision to limit the President's power to make war.

And there is the story of the achievements of Manny and his father in furthering the education of all New Mexicans, a story in its own right as pertinent to the history of the state as the development of the atomic bomb.

* * *

At this point I should perhaps confess my own biases.

My wife, Helen, and I are 4th generation California farmers, our families dating back to the Gold Rush. Retired to an organic farm and orchard in a small rural valley in Northern California, we raise Arab horses, olives, navel oranges, and pecans. Our olive oil has earned local fame, but we have yet to make ends meet as farmers. Helen annually

cares for the many uncared-for old dogs, horses, and feathered creatures as cross our path. We are blessed with bald eagles flying over our farm and the river which borders it. She played a leading role in having Cache Creek, the river that flows through our farm, designated as a wild and scenic river in the mountains above us, and also helped in President Obama's recent establishment of the 330,000+ acre Berryessa Snow Mountain National Monument, to the north and west of our farm. I have accompanied her to hear her testimony on behalf of wildlife and against cruelty towards animals before legislative committees in California, Nevada, and New Mexico. Her quiet yet passionate advocacy before hostile state legislators has brought tears to my eyes.

Since the earliest days of our friendship of nearly 45 years, we have come to love the State of New Mexico, its landscape, wildlife, diverse peoples, and its unique history. It was in 1972, 44 years ago, that I received a call from a complete stranger, Peach Mayer, asking if I would mind her putting me on the New Mexico primary ballot for the presidency. I had no idea that Peach was a good friend of my colleague, Manny Lujan, and his parents. Peach was violently opposed to the Viet Nam War. I had been elected to Congress in 1967, I believe as the first Republican in the House openly opposing the war.

As a Marine, I had seen a little of the terrors of war and the fearful effect of bombing on the people of rural villages in Korea in 1951. I had studied counterinsurgency and Viet Nam for years as a reserve officer, between 1961 and 1967, and I had volunteered for active duty in Viet Nam, when a friend lost a leg there in October, 1965. It had become an obsession with me, as it had with Peach Mayer, to try to end the war, and particularly the bombing, which was creating such devastation in a country nearly as beautiful as California and New Mexico.

Trying to get a symbolic vote against the war in 1972, as Gene McCarthy had in 1968, I barely made a dent in the New Hampshire Presidential primary against Nixon in early March, 1972, getting 19.97% of the vote. I was facing an uphill battle to be re-elected to my Congressional seat in the June California primary. I had no time to go to New Mexico for what was clearly a campaign destined to be lost by a huge margin.

The election in New Mexico, engineered solely by Peach Mayer, however, did have some impact. It led to Manny Lujan having to cast the first Republican vote against the bombing, as my modest few votes (roughly 7%) in the June 6th New Mexico primary election entitled me to one delegate at the Republican National Convention, where Manny Lujan would head his State's delegation.

Years later, Helen and I would buy a small adobe in Madrid, and later still, 120 acres of ranch land on the Galisteo River near Cerrillos. We would become good friends of Peach and Walter Mayer; our properties are at the extreme western edge of the Galisteo Basin, adjacent to the Cerrillos Hills, in the shadow of the Ortiz Mountains. We can look across the river every afternoon at the Southern Pacific Super Chief passing both east and west between Chicago and Los Angeles, the Sangre de Cristo range to the north, and the Jemez Mountains to the northwest.

For nearly 40 years, we have used those properties as

a base for annual explorations of the cliff dwellings and ancient ruins of the Anasazi and later pueblo civilizations. We have been impressed equally by the incomparable Carlsbad Caverns at the southeast corner of the State and the ancient ruins of the Anasazi civilization in Chaco Canyon to the northwest. We have read every history book on New Mexico we could lay our hands on. Some of our favorite writings have been those of authors writing about New Mexico: Willa Cather, Eugene Manlove Rhodes, Tony Hillerman, and Richard Bradford.

We had an interest in Kit Carson for his open fathering of children by Indian women at Taos, his scouting for General Stephen Kearny, and the trek of his Mormon Battalion, en route to an almost crushing defeat in the Mexican War at San Pascual, California. We also, however, formed a great deal of sympathy for the Navajos. The Marine Navajo code-talkers, most of them from New Mexico, saved a lot of Marine lives on Iwo Jima and Okinawa. We felt considerable anger at Carson for his ruthless destruction of the Navajos' peach trees and the massacre at Canyon de Chelly. We loathed his forcing the Navajos on 'The Long Walk' to the Bosque Redondo, with so many dying before they were allowed to return back to their reservation. We read everything we could find on the development of the Santa Fe Trail from Missouri through to Durango in Mexico, and the occupation of New Mexico from the time of the Oñate Expedition of 1598 to Kearny's entrance to Santa Fe in 1846.

We have walked a lot of the countryside trying to find the buried pueblos in the Galisteo Basin, seeking permission of the owners of private lands to view the ancient ruins and the petroglyphs which can be found all over the Basin. Rural New Mexico is a treasure chest of antiquities and history. Its occasional thunderstorms and towering cloud formations are nowhere equaled.

It is fair to say we have come to look on New Mexico as our adopted second State. It is not unlike California, a land of little rain. Its piñon trees are suffering from blight caused by climate change, as are our California oaks. Water has become more precious than the gold and minerals that brought the first settlers to both states. Both states have been blessed with oil and gas reserves that of late have become a matter of both national security and environmental and cultural debate. And both of our incredibly beautiful states have been hurt badly by the urban sprawl that creeps out from our major cities.

It is presumptuous, of course, for a Californian to attempt to write a biography of a New Mexican. Despite assiduous research in the libraries and archives of Santa Fe, there will be many errors that old-time New Mexicans will regard with justifiable concern.

But it still seems a worthwhile effort. The stories of the Lujans and the Mayers in their time need to be preserved, in however imperfect a form.

Ferdinand and Isabella

Chapter 1

The Spanish Colonization of New Mexico, from 1598 to its Occupation by the forces of General Stephen Kearny in 1846

The history of New Mexico starts with the uniting of Spain by the marriage of King Ferdinand of Aragon and Queen Isabella of Castille and their subsequent expulsion of the Moors from Spain in 1942. They shortly afterwards commissioned Christopher Columbus to seek a new route across the Atlantic to the Indies.

Years ago, all California school children were told of Ferdinand and Isabella's sponsorship of Columbus' voyage of discovery in his three ships, the Nina, Pinta, and Santa

Maria in 1492, and the subsequent discovery of what geographer Americus Vespucci would call America. We knew that our Congress had designated October 12th each year as "Columbus Day."

But there our education stopped. We didn't learn until many years later that the Spanish conquests which followed were cruel indeed to the Native Americans. It wouldn't be until the late 20th century that real public doubts began to arise over the mistreatment of Native Americans. Increasing protests by young people and others arose over the honoring of Columbus, the Discoverer, with no mention of Columbus, the Exploiter of the original inhabitants of the Americas. The famed California missionary, Fra Junipero Serra, who accompanied the De Anza expedition into California in 1776, was allotted one of California's two heroic statues in the National Capitol building in Washington D.C. In recent years, however, Serra has come under increasing scrutiny, and historians have identified him as a man of extraordinary cruelty towards the native Californians his priests were forcing to construct the 21 famous missions from San Diego to Sonoma.

It is also only in recent years that we have learned from the advances in archaeology, paleontology and other sciences that native peoples lived in New Mexico long before the famous civilization of the Anasazis between 800 and 1275 A.D. Bones, tools and the points of spears or arrows in the bones of mastodons and other vanished creatures have been discovered which indicate that people may have lived and died in New Mexico for perhaps 12,000 years or more. The ruins of eight pueblos lie in the Galisteo Basin within a few miles of Santa Fe, some yet to be fully excavated and explored.

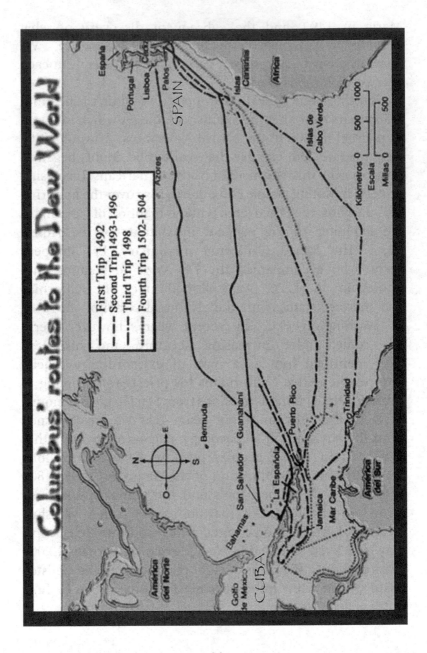

To understand the modern history of New Mexico, therefore, it is well to start back with the times of Columbus.

The discovery of the "New World," with its huge populations of "pagans", in the eyes of the Catholic Church, led the Pope in Rome to designate the King and Queen of Spain as his chosen instrument to spread the Catholic religion to the people found in the Americas and believed by Europeans to be "savages."

In those years, it was deeply believed that the souls of individuals who had not been converted to the Catholic faith were condemned to burn in the fires of Hell. Thus, with the success of Cortez in conquering the Aztecs in Mexico and areas to the south, and Pizarro, in conquering the Incas in Peru, the King of Spain ordered the Conquistadors to escort and support Catholic priests in their "holy mission" of spreading the Catholic religion throughout the New World. Orders like those of the Franciscans, Benedictines, and others furnished hordes of young men of devoted faith and purpose, willing to become martyrs if necessary to save souls.

It was not always clear whether the priests were deemed subject to the military leaders or vice versa. The Spanish King and Queen wanted the native people treated fairly and without cruelty, but the great explorers, from Cortez and Pizarro to Coronado, Oñate, and their successors were fully capable of torture, murder, rape, and massacre. The priests also brought to the Americas the dreaded Inquisition, led by Torquemada in Spain, who felt entitled by God's will to torture and burn men and women at the stake if they did not accept Catholicism and all its beliefs. Any reversion to the worship of the sun, or to rain and corn dances, could result in the cutting off of hands and feet, imprisonment, torture, or even death.

On his second voyage to the New World in 1493,

Columbus brought with him 500 colonists from Spain. From the beginning, despite the wishes of King Ferdinand and Queen Isabella that the natives be treated fairly and kindly, the colonists and Spanish soldiers treated the Indians as savages and often with great cruelty.

The first center of Spanish occupation in the Caribbean was Cuba, and an increasing number of Spanish settlements grew up, as more and more Spaniards immigrated to the New World. There were many courageous young men who hoped to find gold and wealth, not unlike our own people of the gold rushes to California, Nevada, and Montana. More than a few of these men could be brutal to the native Indians with whom they came in contact.

In 1517, the Governor of Cuba, Diego Velazquez, organized the first expedition to what is today Mexico, by Hernando de Cordoba, but he returned empty-handed. A second expedition under Juan de Grijalva in 1518 returned with some gold and news of immense riches inland. In early 1519, a third expedition was organized, but its leader, Hernan Cortez, left Cuba without the Governor's permission, and ultimately reached what is now Mexico City, then the capital of the Aztecs under their ruler, Montezuma. Through trickery and the superiority of his horses, armor, and weapons, Cortez defeated the Aztecs in a series of battles, becoming known as the Great Conquistador. Over the next several years, more and more Spaniards arrived, and in 1536, the King of Spain established a Viceroy as his chief representative. A Council of the Indies was created to serve as Advisors to King Ferdinand and Queen Isabella.

The Viceroy was granted enormous powers, including the granting of encomiendas to Spanish officers. An encomienda could be one or more villages and surrounding lands, with the indigenous inhabitants forced to be the slaves of the grantee.

The discovery of gold, silver, and other precious metals and gems, led to the increasing enrichment of Spain. It also led the rulers of Spain, in compliance with their charge by the Pope in Rome, to feel a deep responsibility to spread Catholicism in the New World. The incredibly valuable cargos being carried back in the galleons of Spain were making the Spaniards the richest nation in Europe. Their empire shortly was to founder with the crushing defeat and dispersal by the English of the Spanish Armada in 1588, which was followed by three centuries of decay. Its once great and wealthy empire ended with the Spanish American War in 1898 with another crushing defeat, by the fledgling nation of the United States.

By virtue of the Mexican War of 1846 and the Spanish-American War of 1898, it can be said that the United States began to build the foundations of a world empire.

In the cases of all three spoils of the Spanish-American War, with the acquisition of the Philippines, Cuba, and Puerto Rico, the American record of conquest and occupation is not one which casts great credit on the United States. As in the case of slavery, which was accepted in our Constitution of 1787, our expansion into areas outside the continental United States, would breed problems and the danger of further warfare.

The Advance of the Conquistadors into New Mexico

In the early 1500's, when the Viceroy was ruling with absolute power in the New World, new expeditions were sent in all directions, hoping to locate new sources of wealth. One such expedition, led by Panfilio Narvaez in 1528, ended in disaster in Florida, with the deaths of most of the Spaniards and their accompanying Franciscan priests and native servants. A few survivors were shipwrecked near what is now Galveston, Texas, there to become the captives of local Indian tribes. Eventually four men escaped, led by Cabeza de Vaca, with two companions and a black Moorish slave, Estevan.

The four wandered, barefoot, and near starvation through Texas and northern Mexico, eventually reaching the west coast and safety amongst Spanish settlers, who helped them reach Mexico City in 1536. During their long period of wandering, they had been befriended and fed by numerous friendly native tribes who told them stories of immensely wealthy Indian settlements to the north. This helped to enhance the legend of the Seven Golden Cities of Cibola, and, in 1539, a Franciscan friar, Marcos de Niza, with Estevan as a guide, led a group north to the villages of the Zuni Indians. Estevan was killed, and de Niza retreated back to Mexico, but told extravagant stories about the rumored rich cities to the north.

As a result, the Governor of the Mexican province of Nueva Galicia, Francisco Coronado, was commissioned to lead 300 soldiers and 800 Indian servants north, reaching the Zuni villages in 1540, and then sending exploration parties both north to Taos and east, to the enormous pueblo at

Pecos, and then further to the east and the great plains of present-day Kansas. No riches were found, and in 1542 Coronado retreated back to Mexico leaving three Franciscans behind who were later killed by the Indians. His armor, horses, and muskets, called arquebuses, were sufficient to overpower such Indian resistance as he had faced, but his cruelties left a lasting impression amongst the Pueblos that Spaniards were to be feared and distrusted.

After Coronado, the Spanish conquistadors were primarily occupied in conquests to the south. It would be nearly 40 years before another expedition went north, led by Captain Francisco Chamuscado and Fray Agustin Rodrigues. They traveled up the Rio Grande valley, reaching the Galisteo Valley just south of present-day Santa Fe, and out into the buffalo plains to the east. Other expeditions ventured north as far as Picuris, but with little success. Although ordered by the Spanish rulers and Viceroy in Mexico City to treat the Indians with courtesy and respect, the Spaniards, starting with Coronado, made demands for food and assistance, and often violated Pueblo women. Thus the first Spaniards were successful in turning many initially friendly indigenous communities into enemies. The Apaches were to become the deadly enemy of the settlers of New Mexico, both Indian and Spaniard.

In 1595, a wealthy colonial leader, Juan de Oñate of Zacatecas, received a contract from the Spanish Crown to colonize the northern frontiers of New Mexico above El Paso. Amongst his group was the first Lujan, a 27-year old native of the Canary Islands, accompanied by an Indian woman who was apparently his servant. Manny Lujan believes she was an Apache.

During the preceding 400 years, a lengthy drought had

*Juan de
Oñate*

led the Anasazi of Chaco Canyon in Northwestern New Mexico, to close up their massive buildings and, over the years, migrate easterly, settling in small communities and ultimately in the pueblos along the Rio Grande.

By the time of Oñate's mission to colonize New Mexico in 1598, there were perhaps as many as 45 or more pueblos in and around the Rio Grande Valley. Earlier large pueblos such as Pueblo Blanco in the Galisteo Basin south of Santa Fe, once occupied with buildings of as many as three stories, with thousands of inhabitants, had been abandoned. In the Galisteo Basin south of Santa Fe, there are eight pueblos within a few miles of each other, all buried beneath the soil, but with petroglyphs found on the surface rocks around them.

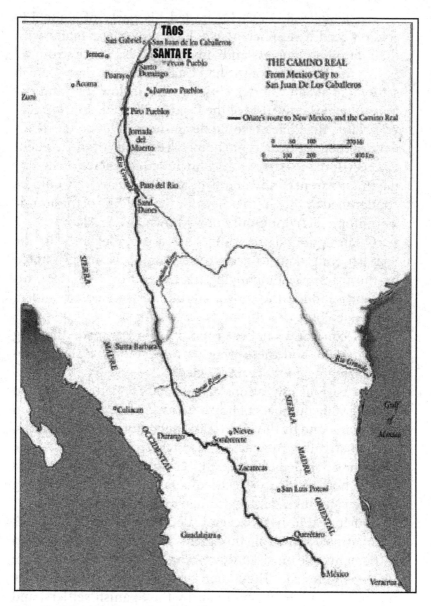

Juan de Oñate's Route to San Gabriel 1598

On January 8, 1598, Oñate led his party of some 129 soldiers and a number of would-be-colonists, many with their families, horses, and other animals, north from El Paso, and in a few months had established the first Spanish settlement at San Gabriel, close to what is now the San Ildefonso Pueblo, at the foot of the Pajarito Plateau. In 1942, 340 years later, the Plateau would be chosen as the secret site for development of the atomic bomb. The lands of the resident Spanish-Indian settlers, which included 310 acres owned by the grandparents and parents of Manuel Lujan Jr., would be condemned by the Government for the building of the atomic laboratory and community now known as Los Alamos.

Oñate required the natives to swear allegiance to the Spanish King, and to accept the religion being promoted by the priests accompanying his expedition. In 1599, his soldiers subdued the rebellious Indians in Acoma, and in other pueblos.

A second and smaller group of colonists made the long trek in 1600, and there were periodic supply trains thereafter, bringing goods from Mexico.

The various migrations of the 1500's and 1600's resulted in increasing numbers of horses roaming free or being stolen by Indians, and by the mid 1600's, neighboring Indian tribes, particularly the Apaches, Comanches, and Kiowas, were becoming skilled horsemen, making increasing raids against both the Spanish settlements and the pueblos, killing the men and taking many women and children as slaves.

During the next several decades following Oñate's occupation, some of the great and prosperous Indian settlements like those at Abo, Gran Quivira, and Quarai were being abandoned. The Indians were becoming increasingly incensed by their ill-treatment by the Spanish settlers, and the Franciscan friars, with their insistence that the native religious rites be replaced by the rules of the Catholic Church. The Spanish Inquisition sent sometimes-vicious priests to police the severe requirements of the Catholic faith and punish those who strayed or sinned, both Spanish and Indian.

The Pueblo Revolt of 1680

For the first 82 years after Oñate, the contests between the appointed Governors of New Mexico, local settlers, and the increasing number of Franciscans sent out to build churches in the various pueblos and convert the Indians, grew increasingly bitter. Some local officials, with the soldiers sent to protect the missionaries, disagreed with the latter's harsh treatment of the Indians. Often they were chastised and threatened by the representatives of the Inquisition for their laxity in enforcing the strict conversion of the Indians. There were constant bitter complaints to the Viceroy in Mexico City by either the appointed Governors or the Spanish priests, contending that their allegedly co-equals were guilty of religious heresy or embezzlement or both.

The great New Mexican cowboy/author at the end of the 19th Century and beginning of the 20th, Eugene Manlove Rhodes, was also a historian of some credentials, and in 1912, in Santa Fe, he published his own version of the story of one of the New Mexican Governors, Don Diego Dionisio de Peñalosa, who served for four years after his predecessor had been removed and punished by the Inquisitors.

A brief summary of Rhodes' story seems worthy of insertion here.

Peñalosa, in the Governor's Palace in Santa Fe in the

early 1660's, was of a mind to treat his native subjects with kindness, and thus drew the wrath of the Inquisition. He was ultimately stripped of his office and honors, disgraced, and forced to parade as a heretic through the streets of Mexico City.

Rhodes recognized that the story of Peñalosa had been told mainly by the religious leaders who persecuted him, and with his typical leaning towards the side of the underdog, told of an incident where Peñalosa observed a new friar, Balthazar Fuentes, gently admonishing a young Indian for doing a rain dance. The powerful representative of Torquemada, the Grand Inquisitor, stormed in, demanding lashes for both the young sinner and the too-lenient priest.

Harsh words were exchanged; the young Indian and priest were only admonished rather than subjected to the lash. Peñalosa extracted a grudging apology from the Inquisitor, who was to later repay him by forcing his removal and subsequent auto da fe, a procedure which often ended in the torture or death at the stake of many alleged heretics. Peñalosa had too many influential relatives to suffer either, but was banished and lived out his life in bitter animosity against both Spain and the Church.

Rhodes has the lenient priest Fuentes escaping to found a religious haven in far off western New Mexico, and become a friend of the hostile Apaches*, while a few years later, the young Indian becomes Popé (Po-pay), the leader of the Pueblo Revolt of 1680, which slew 21 of 33 Franciscan friars in the pueblos, killed hundreds of settlers, and drove the surviving Spanish settlers south to El Paso, where they languished for twelve years until the expedition of a new

---

* *The story of Governor Peñalosa's rise and fall appears as Chapter IX of Rhodes' 1912 book, "West Is West."*

Governor, Captain General Diego de Vargas Zapata Lujan Ponce de Leon y Contreras, returned to re-conquer the colony in 1692.

Diego de Vargas Zapata Lujan Ponce de Leon

When the Pueblo Revolt of 1680 occurred, the Indians drove some 1,000 surviving Spanish settlers and priests south to El Paso. There must have been at least one Lujan who survived the revolt, because in 1692, when de Vargas returned to re-conquer New Mexico, records show that seven Lujans were in the group returning, some of whom settled in Santa Fe, or along the Rio Grande to the north, or in what are now Rio Arriba and Taos Counties.

By 1695, de Vargas had succeeded in the relatively peaceful reconquest of New Mexico, but two hundred years would elapse before the threats of the Apaches, Comanches, Navajos, and Utes would cease to terrify, and on many occasions kill or enslave its inhabitants.

With the power of Spain diminishing, Mexicans revolted in 1821 and obtained their independence, but the people living in New Mexico saw little change in their circumstances by the shift of power from Spain to Mexico. The trail from Mexico City to Santa Fe was over 2,000 miles long, and whether on foot or horseback, involved a great deal of hardship.

Following Lewis and Clark's Exploration of Discovery in 1804-1806, American mountain men in pursuit of beaver pelts began to infiltrate into northern New Mexico, and aggressive traders from Missouri began to travel the famous Santa Fe Trail to Santa Fe, and thence into Mexico.

In 1776, Juan de Anza led an expedition similar to Oñate's into Southern California, and thence up to San Francisco, where he established the San Francisco Presidio, the furthest northern outpost of the still-existing Spanish Empire. But after 1821, the Mexicans would be hard hit to provide settlers and troops to protect their vast northern provinces from Texas to California.

Texans revolted against Mexican rule, and in 1836, established the independence of Texas, leading to the invasion of Mexico by U.S. troops ten years later, achieving victory and the Treaty of Guadalupe Hidalgo in 1848. That treaty brought huge new areas of the Southwest, including California, Arizona, Nevada, and New Mexico under the ownership and rule of the United States.

In 1846, New Mexico had been occupied by U.S. Army forces under General Stephen Kearny. In 1848, New Mexico became a Territory of the United States, with its Hispanic inhabitants entitled to the privileges of U.S. citizenship.

Another 64 years of contention and strife would ensue, however, before New Mexico was admitted to Statehood in 1912. Relationships between the descendants of the original Spanish settlers and the new gringos, bringing cattle and seeking mineral wealth, were not always cordial.

The new State shifted between the control of Republicans and Democrats, and remains today a battleground state where either party may gain control, only to be replaced in the next election. Manuel Lujan Jr., a descendant of the first Lujan to settle in New Mexico, was elected to Congress in 1968 and served with distinction for 20 years in the House of Representatives. In 1989, he was appointed by President George H.W. Bush as Secretary of the Interior. Two distant relatives bearing the name Lujan presently serve in the Congress, and the name Lujan ranks with the most honorable in the State's long history. Despite the long period of cruelty and domination of the natives, both Indian and Hispanic, by the representatives of the Catholic church, there is scarcely a village to be found in New Mexico where the Catholic faith, a sustaining force during the centuries of predation, is not

Chapel at Chimayo

demonstrated by adobe churches that continue to serve the bulk of the local residents.

Nevertheless, it is fairly certain that many of the pueblos continue to unobtrusively practice their historic rites and follow their traditional religious beliefs underground to the present time, even if in secret. Rain dances and corn dances are no longer criminal. After New Mexico became a U.S. territory, there were no longer zealous Catholic priests to overtly punish them for this heresy.

Chapter 2

The Lujan Family Background

It is perhaps not fair to place too much stress on the name Lujan, because under the Spanish system of community property laws, women had many rights equal to men, and Spanish and Mexican history is replete with the names and achievements of a great many women who proved as strong and resilient as the men they married. Of the first Spanish families that were the earliest European settlers of New Mexico, there were many names like Sanchez, Gomez, Gonzales, Otero, Romero, Gallegos, Baca, and Montoya, who may very well have married one or more of the Lujans who rose to political prominence and power in the 20th and 21st centuries.

But as Kathryn Cordova, the chronicler of the modern Lujan generations, wrote, histories have been written primarily by men.

As has been mentioned previously, the first Lujan, Juan Lujan, came to New Mexico in 1598 with the Oñate Expedition. He was 27 and accompanied by an Indian servant.

Church records disclose that a Christopher Lujan was born in 1601, and apparently settled in the Cochiti and Santo Domingo area.

There is mention of a soldier Lujan on a foray against the Apaches in 1623. The first Lujans must have been prolific, because by the time of Governor Rosas in 1640 and the great battles for supremacy between the appointed Governors and the Catholic priests, there is mention of another prominent soldier, Juan Lujan, who perhaps sided with the Governor and was subsequently awarded an encomienda near Taos.

An encomienda was essentially a village or pueblo which was awarded to a conquistador or an officer who had performed particularly valuable services for the leader of a conquering expedition, such as Cortez or Oñate. The residents of the village or pueblo were awarded as slaves. In the early days, officers would petition the King of Spain or his Council of the Indies for encomiendas, contending that they had not been properly compensated for their services. Cortez's famous chronicler, Bernal Diaz, for example, spent a great deal of time and effort petitioning for an award of three villages and their native occupants in Guatemala where he had settled.

In 1680, when the Pueblos rose to throw out the hated Franciscan friars and New Mexican settlers, it is not known how many Lujans were killed. There were several Lujans, however, who were successful in fleeing to El Paso with Governor Otermin.

When Don Diego de Vargas Zapata Lujan Ponce de Leon was authorized to attempt the re-conquest of New Mexico in 1692, there are clear records reflecting that there were at least seven Lujans amongst the group at El Paso who agreed to accompany him in the drive north to retake the capital at Santa Fe. Several Lujans were of great service to him.

It was customary for Conquistadors to send long letters to their superiors, including the Viceroy in Mexico City and the King in Spain, describing the resources of the areas they hoped to pacify and from which they hoped to be able to recover riches to enrich the Spanish Empire, as the conquests of Cortes in Mexico and Pizarro in Peru had done.

In the records of his letters before leaving El Paso, de Vargas mentions an interview with Captain Juan Luis Lujan, an old criollo of Santa Fe, 86 years of age, who had apparently once visited a village of the Moqui (later determined to be Oraibi, one of the Hopi's mesa-top villages far to the northwest of Santa Fe.) Captain Lujan stated he had personally observed two sacks of a reddish ore, believed to be immensely rich, from a mine a day's ride to the west. Captain Lujan estimated that, because of the Apaches and Havasupai, it would require an armed force of 100 fully-armed Men at Arms, each with 12 horses and 6 mules (to carry his suit of armor), to reach the mine and recover its riches.

When de Vargas wrote about his re-conquest of New Mexico in 1692, he listed among his fairly small group of soldiers, 15 men from the Presidio of Cerro Gordo, including one Juan Lujan, each man "fully armed with 8 horses, gunpowder, and bullets."

The extra horses were a necessity to carry the heavy armor, weapons, ammunition, and other equipment which made the heavily-armored Spanish horsemen the victors in their many fights with the poorly-armed Indians.

There is an amusing story here worth recounting, if only to describe the problems of the settlers, and the burdens on an American cavalryman facing the Apaches. In 1852, shortly after New Mexico became a territory of the United States, Indian Agent John Greiner wrote a letter, presumably to his superiors in Washington:

> "There are 92,000 Indians (estimated) in this Territory. Many of them are at war. We have not 1,000 troops here under Colonel Sumner to manage them. Our troops are of no earthly account. They cannot catch a single Indian. A Dragoon mounted will weigh 225 pounds. Their horses are all as poor as carrion. The Indians have nothing but their bow and arrows

*and their ponies are as fleet as deer. Cipher it up.
Heavy dragoons on poor horses, who know nothing
of the country, sent after Indians at home anywhere,
and who always have some hours start, how long will
it take to catch them? So far, although several expeditions have been sent after them, not a single Indian has
been caught."*

At one point, after de Vargas' group of 700 settlers and
less than 100 soldiers had reached the outskirts of Santa Fe,
to find it fully occupied by hostile Indians, de Vargas' people
became desperate for food. Miguel Lujan became a hero
when he brought in five wagonloads of maize (corn) from the
pueblos around Santa Fe. While the Indians still occupied
the City, a message came to de Vargas from a soldier, Miguel
Lujan, that the Indians were planning to attack and massacre
soldiers and settlers. The message led de Vargas to prepare
for battle with the cry: "Santiago, Santiago, Death to these
Rebels," and after several years the de Vargas re-conquest of
New Mexico was successful, albeit with much violence and
brutality against the Indians.

The Modern Lujan Family

Manuel Lujan Sr. and Lorenzita Lujan

The modern Lujan family starts with Manny's great grandfather, Manuel Antonio Lujan y Sanchez, who lived from 1829 to 1898, and according to family lore, was working on the first dirt road up to Los Alamos when a boulder broke loose and rolled over him, causing his death.

His son, Martin Lujan, Manny's grandfather, was born in 1869 in San Ildefonso, married Zenaida Sanchez, and settled a homestead on the Pajarito Plateau of 160 acres, where his son, Manuel Lujan Sr., later bought 150 adjoining acres where both raised beans, corn, oats, wheat, and other crops until the United States Government condemned their lands to build the secret Los Alamos Laboratory in 1942. Martin Lujan also had a small farm adjacent to the Pueblo of Santa Fe, where he operated a mill and small grocery store. In the late 1920's, he moved to Santa Fe and opened another grocery store, which was very successful. When Manny Jr. reached the age of 21, his grandfather loaned him $500 to buy his first car, requiring only that the 10% interest be paid on time, with no due date for the principle. He died in 1955.

Manny's father, Manuel Lujan Sr., born in 1893 at San

Manuel Lujan Sr. with the first class he taught at San Ildefonso Pueblo

Ildefonso, was a special man, a leader in every field he entered. He became not only a successful educator, farmer, rancher, and businessman, but enjoyed a political career which led him in his later years to be honored by the Republicans of New Mexico as the revered "Mr. Republican."

The remarkable story of Manuel Lujan Sr. and his wife Lorenzita, is perhaps as much a story of the rise of Hispanic Americans of New Mexico to national recognition as it is of their lives together.

Of limited early education, but continuing to self improve his education and abilities well into middle age,

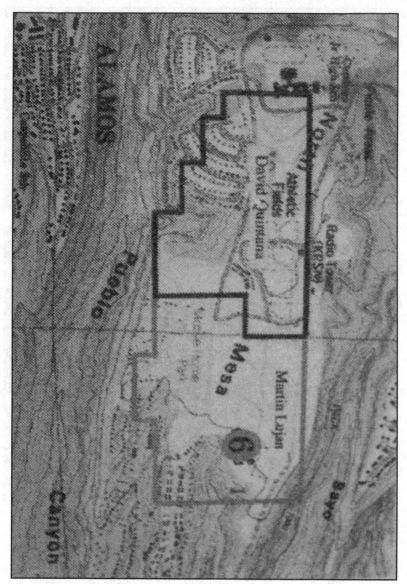

Lands of the Lujans condemned in 1943 for Los Alamos Laboratory.

Family tradition always remained important to the Lujan clan.
Two "generation photos" represented the ideal of honoring the family's
heritage. The first photo featured the following Lujan men: Martin,
Manuel Sr., Manuel Jr., and on his father's lap, Tommy. The second picture
shows the first born of each generation: Frank Marchi, Manuel Lujan Jr.,
Manuel Lujan Sr., and Martin Lujan.

Manuel Lujan Sr. started as a farmer, served as a teacher of the children of San Ildefonso Pueblo, became a school principal, married one of his school teachers, Lorenzita Romero, started a large family, moved that family to Santa Fe at the age of 33 and started in the insurance business.

MAYOR of SANTA FE
REPUBLICAN CANDIDATE FOR CONGRESS

At the age of 32, the Republican Party of Santa Fe County asked him to run for County Assessor in 1926, a post he occupied for four years.

In those days, education of the largely Hispanic community in Northern New Mexico lagged far behind other parts of the United States. But in 1932 and again in 1934, at the height of the Depression, Manuel Sr. was elected as the Santa Fe Superintendent of Schools. During the difficult Depression years, he developed his insurance business in Santa Fe, joined by several of his children and their spouses. In 1942, assisted by his 14-year-old son, Manuel Jr., he was elected Mayor of Santa Fe. In that same year, his wife, Lorenzita, after bearing eleven children, was elected County Clerk of Santa Fe County. It would be hard to find a better success story in any part of America.

It could well be said of Manuel Lujan Sr. and his wife that they, with the help of their friends, Katharine and Walter Mayer and others, created a new sense of honesty

Manuel Sr. accompanied by his grandchildren.

and integrity in a Republican Party which, like its Democrat counterpart, had been accustomed to corruption, vote-buying and other chicanery since New Mexico was first occupied in 1846 by General Kearny.

As heads of a large family, the Lujans were devout Catholics, celebrating mass and taking communion daily in their home at 858 West Manhattan Street. Tragedy struck them when two beautiful older daughters died in the flower of their young womanhood, and two male babies died in infancy. The Lujans lived to see seven of their children become eminently successful, with one going on to Congress and ultimately to serve four years as Secretary of the Interior.

Their oldest son, Manuel Jr., was required to work hard in his youth, and his parents set him a clear example of the virtues of honesty and participation in public service. They were proud to have him help them in both civic and church activities, as well as the family insurance business.

Manuel Lujan Sr., although increasingly successful in building what would become Santa Fe's largest privately-owned insurance company, retained his interest in education and farming. Until he sold their last farm near Moriarty in 1957, his children, even as newlyweds like Manuel Jr. and his wife Jean, were required to spend weekends helping their parents on the farm. Their father's sale of that farm came as a happy event in their lives.

Manuel Sr. ran unsuccessfully for Congress in 1946, losing to the incumbent Clinton Anderson, and in 1948, was defeated for the Governorship of New Mexico, although credible rumors that the election was stolen have persisted over the years.

Manuel Jr., as an assistant in his father's campaign for Governor, personally observed an interesting example of integrity on his father's part. Journeying to the recreational center of Ruidoso, a leader in the gaming industry approached the candidate and promised him a check for $7,500 a month during his anticipated two-year term in office, if he would allow the gambling interests to continue their profitable businesses.

The Gubernatorial candidate turned him down flat. His son, when he became Secretary of the Interior, similarly turned down any propositions in which he suspected bad motives might lurk.

Even though he lost, Manuel Lujan Sr. had become a recognized political power in his own right, and in 1951, was appointed by the Governor to the important post of Commissioner of Revenue.

But Manuel Sr. remained a farmer and educator at heart. He never lost his dedication to the improvement of the education of New Mexican children. The lack of basic educational facilities for the descendants of the first Spanish settlers was a constant concern, and his success in ameliorating that problem during his lifetime would constitute both a legacy and inspiration for his son, Manuel Jr., in his later career of public service.

The Preparation of Manuel Lujan, Jr.
for High Office

In 1940, from the age of 12 on, there were plenty of employment opportunities for young boys in Santa Fe. Manny Jr. started helping his father in the insurance business, delivering papers and policies, and doing other chores. He attended Guadalupe School and then St. Michael's High School. He worked hard at ranch and farm chores for his father, who was a business partner of Peach Mayer's husband.

After a year at St. Mary's College in Moraga, California, he became homesick for his childhood sweetheart, Jean, and returned to finish at St. Michael's College, in 1950 getting a degree in business management. He and Jean married, she at 18, he at 21.

Manny worked at various jobs. He clerked in a clothing store, and for a wholesale fruit and vegetable business, unloaded freight cars with merchandise headed for Los Alamos, loaded and unloaded trucks with cases of Coca Cola, and finally started working in his father's insurance business.

He attended a school in insurance and wrote his first policy, earning a commission of less than $150 just in time to pay his wife's hospital bill after the birth of their first child. It was a family custom for the Lujans and their brothers-in-law to build their own homes. Manny remodeled an old adobe house on his parents' property for the first home of his own, and ten years later built a three bedroom adobe, in the meantime helping his brothers-in-law build houses as they had helped him. He and Jean lived there for ten years before moving to Albuquerque to start his own insurance business with his brother.

*Lujan and family working on election campaign. Manuel Sr. and
Lorenzita on the left. Manuel Jr. is in the center.*

Meanwhile, he had continued to be active in his father's
various political campaigns, and helping with local church
and party activities. By his 39th birthday in 1967, he had
built a successful business and was ready for greater things.

A good deal of his education had come from a special
couple in Santa Fe, his father's ranching and farming partner,
Walter Mayer, and his wife, Katharine "Peach" Mayer, who
had worked for many years in Republican politics with
Manny's father.

Chapter 3

1967, The Year of Decision
Manuel Lujan Jr. and
Peach and Walter Mayer

In 1967, Manuel Lujan Jr. was at the peak of health and a successful business career. He had, since his youth, given a great deal of service to his political party. He had adhered to Abraham Lincoln's admonition: "Study and get ready and then the chance will come."

One day he got a call that would be life-changing. The Chairman of the state Republican Party called him to advise that a poll showed the incumbent Congressman for the First Congressional District to be vulnerable. Would Manny consider running?

The Republican Party of New Mexico had a long and tawdry record since becoming a U.S. territory in 1848. Its history was particularly disreputable in the days of the infamous "Santa Fe Ring," which had held sway from after the Civil War until the early years of Statehood. Both U.S. Senators, T. B. Catron and Albert B. Fall, were members of the Ring. It was made up of greedy businessmen, land speculators and railroad entrepreneurs, all interested in acquiring such lands and whatever wealth they could at the expense of the settlers and native Americans. They were primarily Republicans.

One of the best of the short stories by Eugene Manlove Rhodes related to the only time a Democrat had been elected in the early days in Socorro County. It was published in the <u>Saturday Evening Post</u> of April 8, 1911, and entitled "*A Number of Things*". There had not been a Democrat official elected in the memory of living man. It required the public disclosure of the ineptitudes and deceit of the incumbent sheriff, district attorney, and judge to elect a Democrat sheriff.

In the early days there had been an honest Republican Governor, Octaviano Larrazolo, who was the first Hispanic elected to the U. S. Senate in 1928. There had been another Republican, Bronson Cutting, elected to the Senate in 1928 and re-elected in 1934, despite the Roosevelt landslide that year. Cutting, a Harvard classmate of FDR, was the wealthy owner and sometimes editor of the Santa Fe New Mexican. Unfortunately, he died that year shortly after the 1934 election in a plane crash.

There would be a succession of Democrat Senators, Dennis Chavez, Clinton Anderson, and Joseph Montoya. But in 1967, there were no New Mexico Republicans holding national office.

The First Congressional District was predominantly Democrat in registration, but also heavily Hispanic. Only in Bernalillo County, where Albuquerque was situated, were Hispanics in the minority.

Manny was fluent in both English and Spanish. He had a great base of friends in Santa Fe from St. Michael's High School and his later graduation from St. Michael's College. His father, Manuel Sr., was the beloved "Mr. Republican" of New Mexico. Manny had done yeoman work at every level of political action, working up the Republican ladder of responsibility and being elected as state Party Vice President.

He had moved his insurance business to Albuquerque to take advantage of the greater market possibilities there. He enlisted in the National Guard in 1948, and knew many of the guardsmen. He had been fortunate that the Guard was not called up during the Korean War.

The fact that the First District had a majority of Democratic voters was a challenge, but a lot of those Democrats
were Manny's friends.

Would Manny take up the challenge? Why not? He
decided to run.

But despite his business success, he was not wealthy. He
would need money.

Here enters Katharine Van Stone "Peach" Mayer,
undoubtedly the leading lady of Republican politics in Santa
Fe, if not the whole state, for some years.

Katharine "Peach" Mayer, and
her husband, Walter

Peach was a native New Mexican, a Phi Beta Kappa
graduate of Colorado College. She had been involved in
politics from her precinct to the White House.

Her first involvement had been as a young social worker
in the 1930s, watching Democrats give preference in handing
out benefit checks to fellow Democrats. And so she chose to
become a Republican.

She had earned impeccable credentials as a Republican
by 1967. She had been a supporter of Wendell Willkie in
1940 and the Co-Chairperson of Republicans for Dwight
Eisenhower in 1952 and 1956, and a pledged delegate for
Barry Goldwater at the Republican Convention in San Francisco in 1964, although she preferred Nelson Rockefeller.

She had worked for and with her friend, Manuel Lujan
Sr., in Republican campaigns for over 30 years. Although
Manuel Sr. was scrupulously honest, he and Peach had an
easy working familiarity with the seamier elements of Santa

Fe, a town which had been wide open from before and after the days of General Kearny's arrival in 1846. After all, gamblers and the women of houses of ill fame generally voted. One of the most famous houses, since torn down, was located across the street from the Boy's Club.

Peach had been a civic leader in all sorts of causes, serving on several state boards and the boards of local charities, and working on financial matters for the world-famous Santa Fe Opera.

Katharine "Peach" Mayer

Walter Mayer

She was renowned for her intelligence, beauty, and political acumen.

She had good contacts among wealthy Republicans around the state and fundraising was one of the political activities at which she was adept.

She also had uncanny political instincts. She had many Democrat friends, and didn't hesitate to vote for Democrats she liked. In early 1976, she was

Walter and Peach Mayer and sons. Tom Mayer, her preferred delegate to the 1972 Republican convention, is on the right.

asked by another friend, ace New York Times reporter, R. W. "Johnny" Apple, if she would convene a group of New Mexico's leading Democrats to take a poll on whom they thought would be the Democratic candidate for the White House. Peach held a dinner party at her house, close by the State Capitol, for a group of the State's Democrat leaders, which included the sitting Governor and a former Governor. They went around the table, none of them giving any credence to Jimmy Carter. Johnny Apple then asked Peach what she thought. "I like that nice man from Georgia," she said. "I'll bet any of you he wins your nomination, and I'll also bet he'll be elected." One of the Governors was a strict Baptist, but the other, a gambling man, said "Peach, I love you and I don't want to take your money."

She was friends with many nationally-prominent

Republicans, men like Chief Justice Warren Burger and Senator Prescott Bush.

In 1952 and 1956, she had been obliged to work with Richard Nixon, a man she grew to intensely dislike. In 1967, when Nixon was gearing up for his 1968 presidential campaign, he called her and asked her if she would do for him in New Mexico what she had done for Eisenhower in 1952 and 1956.

"Dick," she said, "I'm flattered. I'd be delighted to, on one condition."

"What's that?" Nixon asked. She answered: "You give me a written signed statement, promising me that you'll end the war within six months of your inauguration. I give you my word I won't mention it or show it to anyone unless you break your promise."

Needless to say, Nixon didn't want to pin himself down to anything in writing, then or later. He campaigned, promising a secret plan to end the war. It turned out to be a plan he devised with Henry Kissinger to quadruple the bombing, not just in Viet Nam, but secretly in Laos and Cambodia as well. That bombing would turn the Mayers, as it did me, into being passionate advocates to end the bombing.

In mid-1969, Peach had mounted a cork board with pictures of Nixon, Haldeman, and Ehrlichman over her desk. She would amuse herself by throwing darts at them.

A lot of famous people had been honored to be her dinner guests at her home: Greer Garson, Igor Stravinsky, Donald Gramm, Vera Zorina, Goddard Lieberson, Witter Bynner, and Wallace Stegner, among others.

Her husband, Walter, was a rancher who had come to Santa Fe for relief from lung disease stemming from his being seriously wounded and gassed at the Argonne in World War

I. He was a great man in his own right. Once he felt he had recovered from his disabilities from the war, although he was given a 100% disability rating, Walter returned his check to the Government. Walter, a partner in ranching and farming with Manuel Lujan Sr., rather despised politics and politicians but had been elected to the City Council with Manuel Sr. in 1942 and appointed as Fire and Police Commissioner. He had also been the mentor of young Manuel Jr. in his youth in the livestock business and irrigated farming. They had become fast friends.

Walter Mayer, as Police Commissioner, didn't feel strongly about Santa Fe's historic "wide open town" designation, but as young soldiers began to appear in the area in 1943 to protect the "secret" goings on at Los Alamos, Walter took steps to protect them. The main house of ill fame in Santa Fe was across from the Boys Club. Walter called in the madams and their charges and issued a stern warning: "I'm not going to interfere with your businesses if you keep yourselves clean and have medical checks each week. But if I hear of any of the GI's getting venereal disease, I'll shut you down forthwith."

His words were heeded. Santa Fe prospered and the soldiers got through the war.

So it was therefore entirely right and appropriate, once he had made the decision to run for Congress in 1967, that Manny approach Peach and Walter for their advice and support.

Manuel was living in Albuquerque. He made an appointment to meet with Peach, and drove the 60-plus miles to Santa Fe to see her. He was wearing a somewhat stained necktie. He inquired if she might possibly be willing to intervene on his behalf with one of Santa Fe's richest citizens, Marshall McCune.

McCune was fond of Peach and was accustomed to making financial contributions to candidates suggested to him by Peach. But he was no soft touch.

Manny waited nervously at Peach's side when she called McCune to plead Manny's case. "Why the hell should I give him any money?" said the crusty philanthropist. "He's not his father." "Because you believe in the two-party system," Peach replied.

Her charm carried the day. McCune agreed to see her young man.

Whereupon Peach yanked off the stained necktie and replaced it with one of her husband's or son's, tying it herself and sending Manny on his way. McCune came through with a substantial contribution, enough to get Manny's campaign off to a good start.

Manny ran, campaigned hard, and in a startling upset, won. His victory was thought by many observers to be the greatest miracle of all time in New Mexican politics.

He would join some 60 other young Republican women and men in their first or second terms in the House of Representatives in January, 1969, to be welcomed with open arms. I was one of them. Our acknowledged leader was George H.W. Bush, the first Republican elected from Texas since Reconstruction. Many of us would campaign for Bush when he left the House in 1970 to run for the Senate in an unsuccessful race against Lloyd Bentsen.

I had been asked by Wisconsin Senator Gaylord Nelson to Co-Chair the first Earth Day with him on April 22, 1970. Bush was trying to convince Texas voters that he would be a great environmentalist, and he asked me to go up in a dirigible over Houston with a group of reporters to view the Houston ship channel, then boasting varying colors of green, brown, red, and yellow, returning to hold a press conference where he solemnly announced that, if elected, he would clean up the badly polluted waterway. It was impressive but not enough to defeat the popular Bentsen.

Earth Day had an unexpected result. The young people who sponsored teach-ins about environmental issues around the country in 1970, joined to form a political action group, Environmental Action, and labeled twelve House Members as "The Dirty Dozen." They then organized turn-out-the-vote efforts in their home districts, astonishingly defeating seven of the twelve, one being Walter Fallon, Chairman of the powerful Public Works or "pork" committee who was accustomed to do favors for Members by granting funds for projects in their Districts.

The defeat of seven incumbents by those who had been contemptuously referred to as "only a bunch of kids," had an enormous impact.

When Congress convened in January, 1971, there were a great many new dedicated environmentalists. This resulted in passage of a number of landmark environmental laws: the Clean Air, Clean Water, and Endangered Species Acts among them. Nearly all of them were co-sponsored by Manny Lujan.

Manny would be seriously challenged for re-election only once in the next two decades, in 1980, when he was vastly outspent by fellow Hispanic, Bill Richardson, whom Manny narrowly defeated by a little over 50% to 49%.

Chapter 4

The Special Educational Needs of the First Congressional District in 1968

By January, 1969, when Manuel Lujan Jr. was sworn into Congress, the City of Santa Fe where he had grown up and been educated was a thriving cosmopolitan small city, home to a mixed population perhaps half to two-thirds Hispanic. It had long been a haven for sufferers from tuberculosis, pneumonia, and other lung diseases, known for its clear mountain air at 7,000 foot elevation, snuggled at the base of the beautiful Sangre de Cristo mountains. A number of retired millionaires had come to town, many to build spacious adobe homes with all the modern conveniences.

Santa Fe had also become a major tourist attraction with its Native Americans selling sought-after authentic rugs, blankets, pottery, and jewelry on one side of the historic Plaza, and the historic La Fonda hotel on the other. It had become a world-renowned center of the arts, with a host of painters, writers, musicians, holistic healers and people of strong independent minds coming from Chicago, Hollywood, Texas, and other places. Its celebrations of Holy Saint Days, the banishing of gloom in the annual Zozobra celebration, and the native dances at the pueblos were attended by thousands of out-of-town visitors. There was a thriving gay community, well ahead of its time, its leading member perhaps Peach's friend, the famous poet, Hal Brynner.

There had been a major transformation of the State by the decision of the federal government in 1942 to condemn the lands on the remote Pajarito Plateau, some 25 miles to

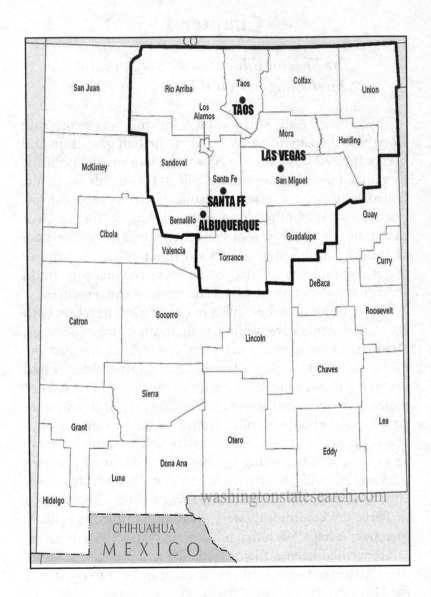

The 1st Congressional District in 1968.

the northwest for a secret laboratory for the building of the first atomic bomb. The 310 acres of the agricultural lands of Manny's grandfather and father had been taken for the project. The family would not receive proper compensation for over 50 years.

The Atomic Bomb

Albert Einstein had advised President Roosevelt of his belief that the Nazis were creating a nuclear fission bomb, the power of which could revolutionize warfare. The President had directed the consolidation of all atomic research under a single agency, the project to develop an atomic bomb and given the name "The Manhattan Project." Dozens of the world's best scientists, men like the Italian, Enrico Fermi, from the University of Chicago, Hans Bethe, an immigrant from Norway, Nels Bohr of Denmark, and Edward Teller, a Hungarian came to Santa Fe. Nobel prize winners and the best physicists came from American universities such as Princeton, M.I.T. and the University of California, all arriving by train or car, to report to the secret headquarters at 109 East Plaza, under false names, there to be transported up the winding two lane road to Los Alamos. The office at 109 East Plaza was run by a good friend of the Mayers, Dorothy "Dink" McKibben.

Unknown at the time, one of the British scientists, Klaus Fuchs, would serve periodically as a weekly conduit of the developing designs and plans for the bombs to a Russian agent at the foot of the Pajarito Plateau.

From 1942 on, the Manhattan Project was a race to beat the Nazis. By July, 1945, the Americans had won, too late to use the bomb against Hitler's Germany, but in time to

bring an early end to the war with Japan with the dropping of bombs in early August, 1945, first on Hiroshima and a few days later on Nagasaki.

Several hundred thousand Japanese died, and thousands more were condemned to slow and painful deaths, but the war ended. It is sometimes forgotten that the bomb may have saved the lives of a million American soldiers scheduled to land on Japan's main islands in November, 1945, and perhaps also the lives of 10 million Japanese, pledged under the Shinto philosophy to die rather than surrender. The Japanese had demonstrated that willingness many times in the bloody fighting after the Marines started the advance north from Guadalcanal, Guam and Saipan, Iwo Jima and finally Okinawa.

Hundreds of Japanese civilians had jumped to their deaths off the cliffs into the sea rather than surrender to the American forces. When Harry Truman made the fateful decision to use the bomb so painfully created at Los Alamos, it may have been the most difficult decision of his or any other presidency. Truman had served in the American Expeditionary Force in World War I and had seen the horrors, misery, and suffering of the wounded and the dying.

The decision to use the bomb will always be a matter of strong controversy. I was 17 at the time and a lot of my friends were in the Army and Marine units being marshaled for the scheduled November, 1945, invasion of the Japanese home islands. It is fair to say that they, and their friends and loved ones breathed a great collective sigh of relief, as the Emperor of Japan finally agreed to an unconditional surrender in August, 1945.

Many of the scientists who participated in the bomb's creation suffered pangs of conscience, and the Union of Concerned Scientists was formed to try to prevent its use ever again. Whether they will be successful remains a matter of conjecture. I confess to an uneasy feeling that sooner or later some ruthless person will get possession of, and detonate, a bomb in one or more of our larger cities. Our arrogance in using guided missiles, blockbuster bombs, and unarmed drones against civilian targets around the world have created a lot of enemies willing to die to kill Americans.

The impact of the Manhattan Project was not limited to Los Alamos and its environs. The White Sands were taken for use as the testing place for the new invention. Alamagordo was turned into a major defense center. The ranch of writer Eugene Manlove Rhodes was included in a huge new area for the testing of rockets and other missiles. The Lawrence Laboratories, in California, were linked with the new Sandia Laboratory in Albuquerque, and facilities for New Mexican universities for the training of new scientists were substantially increased. Los Alamos, springing up suddenly as it did, became perhaps the wealthiest new small city in New Mexico and remains so today. Only recently, there was a public announcement that the Los Alamos and Sandia Laboratories have been granted a contract to build a newly-designed trigger mechanism for our arsenal of atomic weapons, a contract that will take until 2020 to complete.

But for the native New Mexicans, educational opportunity and health care in the First Congressional District north of Los Alamos did not materially change by the new position of New Mexico as center of scientific research and development of the fission, and later fusion, bombs.

The citizens of the northern counties were predominantly Hispanic, with many barely getting by in subsistence farming, or on sheep and cattle ranches, still without the educational benefits that existed elsewhere in the nation. There were few schools beyond the elementary level, and many children dropped out before their high school years. Spanish was still the language spoken in the homes. There was a high rate of illiteracy, infant mortality, and poverty.

Mora County was the poorest county in the State. In 1940, its Hispanic population was 96%, closely followed by the counties of Rio Arriba and Taos at 95%, Sandoval and San Miguel at 83% and Valencia at 81%. Santa Fe County was at 67%, and even Bernalillo and Torrance counties were at 53% and 48%, respectively. These nine counties were at the very heart of the First Congressional District.

In 1940, a Professor at the University of New Mexico, Dr. George Sanchez, had written a book, *"The Forgotten People,"* lamenting the fact that the descendants of the original Spanish settlers had survived in spite of a complete lack of education, other than religious instruction by the Catholic priests. There had been no help from the Spanish government during the nearly two centuries of colonization, and after Mexico achieved independence in 1821, the government in Mexico City had offered no help whatsoever.

It would be two years after General Kearny took possession of New Mexico in 1846, before New Mexico achieved status as a territory of the United States, and not until 1912 would New Mexico be admitted to Statehood.

While Dr. Sanchez had described the dismal state of the forgotten people of Northern New Mexico in 1940, he wrote a Forward for a second edition in 1967, indicating that not much had changed since 1940.

Sanchez quoted at length from an 1847 address made by Governor Donaciano Vigil to the first Legislative Assembly after the United States had taken possession. He made a strong plea for improving education.

For its historic value, I will quote parts of Vigil's address here:

> *"It is only through the diffusion of knowledge that a people are enabled to follow the example of those nations whose wise policy shows itself in the higher intelligence and happiness of their people. The world generally is progressive, and how can we avail ourselves of the advancement unless the people are educated?"*

Governor Vigil went on to state some basic concepts which the American people could well re-examine in this year of political disarray.

> *"If your government here is to be republican, if it is to be based upon democratic-republican principles, and if the will of the majority is to be one day*

the law of the land and the government of the people, it is evident for this will to be properly exercised, that the people must be enlightened and instructed. And it is particularly important in a country where the right of suffrage is accorded and secured to all, that all should be instructed and that every man should be able to read to inform himself of the passing events of the day and of the matters interesting to his country and government. This is the age of improvement, both in government and society and it more particularly becomes us, when commencing, as it were, a new order of things, to profit by and promote such improvements, and they can only be encouraged and promoted by diffusing knowledge and instruction among the people. The diffusion of knowledge breaks down antiquated prejudices and distinctions, introduces the people of all countries to a more intimate and attached acquaintance, and is calculated to cultivate these sympathies among the masses in all nations which induce comparison and insure improvement. The world at large is advancing and how can we profit by the advance unless the people are educated? It is true that the available means which could be applied at present to the cause of education are small, but for the promotion of so desirable an object they might be both increased and economized. All that the Legislature can do in the cause of education for the people is most earnestly pressed upon them and will meet with my hearty approval and cooperation."

A historian, Dr. Ralph Emerson Twitchell, in his "The Military Occupation of New Mexico," wrote about Vigil:

"Governor Vigil was found on the side of the people as against the imperious exactions and oppression of the priests as well as against those of the politicians, both of whom were alike resting as an incubus upon the country in 1848, rock-rooted and moss-grown, in contradistinction of the most sacred principles and privileges of humanity, by the authority and prestige of nearly three centuries of church and state combined."

Dr. Sanchez, in his 1967 Preface to the 2nd edition of *"The Forgotten People,"* wrote that even with FDR's New Deal programs and Lyndon Johnson's War on Poverty, the circumstances of the natives of Northern New Mexico had not changed all that much since New Mexico had been admitted to statehood. They remained much like a Spanish colony in an increasingly wealthy New Mexican environment. There had been attempts to improve the situation with small new schools in Las Vegas, Española and Santa Fe, but they had not done much to ameliorate the problems of the children in the generally impoverished northern counties.

This was an injustice Manny's father had spent most of his life attempting to redress, moving from teacher at the San Ildefonso Pueblo, to school principal, to Santa Fe County Supervisor of Education. It was a situation his son, Manny Jr., would face as well. He hoped to do what he could in Congress to improve the circumstances of the people he would represent.

He would have the opportunity to do so in his subcommittees of the Interior Committee. In many respects he would be successful.

Chapter 5

Manuel Lujan Jr. Goes to the House of Representatives

In November, 1968, the nation celebrated the election of Richard Nixon, a man who said he had a plan to end the war in Viet Nam. Viet Nam was still thought to be a "good" war in the eyes of most Americans who wanted to trust him. Nearly all Republican members of the Congress shared that common belief... that it was a war necessary to prevent a lot of other small countries in Southeast Asia from falling like dominoes to the dread spectre of Stalin's desire to have communism dominate the world.

In late 1967, I had gone to the House of Representatives as the first Republican elected opposing the war. It stemmed from my experiences in the Korean War and from years of study of counterinsurgency tactics as a Marine reserve officer, culminating in words of a friend from his hospital bed at the Oak Knoll Naval Hospital's amputee ward. My friend, a gung-ho regular Lieutenant Colonel, had commanded one of the first battalions of Marines to land at Danang to protect the million-dollar South Vietnamese fighter bombers at the Danang airfield. He had stepped on a buried .105 shell while watching his troops maneuver against a small village from which rockets had been fired at the airfield. He told me in October, 1965, that we couldn't win the minds and hearts of the Vietnamese people while burning down their villages. His message proved only too true, but it was one I found myself unable to successfully convey to either my constituents or my colleagues in the Congress, like Manny.

The War in Viet Nam had been sold to the Congress and the American people, in 1964, as a war intended to help the South Vietnamese people fight off communism.

It would not be until June, 1971, that the New York Times would publish the *Pentagon Papers*, and the American people would be shocked to learn that their sons were dying 10% to support the South Vietnamese, 20% to hold off the Chinese, and 70% to save American face. This was the opinion of the Assistant Secretary of Defense, Robert McNaughton, rendered to his boss, Robert McNamara. Americans dying to save face, rather than help South Vietnamese, was not a position most politicians could defend any longer.

With the publication of the *Pentagon Papers*, Peach Mayer's concerns suddenly became those of a majority of the American people, and the 1972 elections would send a majority to Congress dedicated to ending the bombing.

But all this was unknown in 1968 to Manuel Lujan, Jr. when he arrived in Washington, there to join some 60 other young Republicans in their first and second terms, with the drunks and scoundrels fewer than the usual numbers that had served in the House since the First Congress.

Manny would learn speedily, as I had a year earlier, that freshman Republicans were best seen and not heard and that it would take years before they could hope to be on the most powerful committees: Rules, Appropriations, and Ways and Means. It would be six years before he would be appointed to the prestigious Joint Committee on Atomic Energy, despite having the famous Los Alamos Laboratory in the heart of his District.

He would quickly learn the reality that it could be several years before an amendment he might offer to a bill would be respectfully heard. He learned that a freshman of the minority party might rate a one on a scale where the Speaker rated a 1,000 and Chairs of the powerful Appropriations, Rules, and Ways and Means Committees perhaps 900, the Chair of the Armed Services Committee 800 and Chairs of other committees and subcommittees ranging between 300 and 700. Freshman Democrats might well be considered a 10. But the reality was brought home forcibly that while each of the 435 Members had one vote, that vote would ultimately be cast only on bills sponsored by Democrats and chosen by the top leaders in the House to be worthy of consideration.

Minority Members, of which Manny would be one for his entire 20 years in Congress, if they were honest and respectful as Manny was, would be listened to in the subcommittee and committee hearings where the real work was done in the preparation of legislation, and on occasion permitted to offer amendments of corrective language. But they would never have their names on a bill, like the Taft Hartley Act or the Smoot Hawley Tariff in 1930, which had doomed Republicans for the following twenty-two years.

There were few Republicans I knew who were as respected by Republicans and Democrats alike, for his quiet and thoughtful approach to the making of laws to guide the nation. Manny generally voted as the Republican leadership suggested, but he remained totally respected on both sides of the aisle.

We had a lot of political hacks in both parties, but there were a lot of good people as well. Our leaders, Gerry Ford, Bob Michel, John Rhodes, and John Anderson were men of high quality. People like Republicans Barber Conable and Brownie Reid of New York, Jim Leach of Iowa, Jim Johnson and Don Brotzman of Colorado, Bill Steiger of Wisconsin, Pete Biester and Jack Heinz of Pennsylvania, Paul Findley of Illinois, Joel Pritchard of Washington, Jerry and Shirley Pettis of California, George H.W. Bush of Texas, along with Democrats Mo Udall of Arizona, Dave Obey of Wisconsin, Barbara Jordan of Texas, and Don Edwards, George Miller, Norm Mineta and Leon Panetta of California were names which come readily to mind as examples of great political ability, highly respected by their peers.

Coming from a state which received 25% of its budget from oil and gas revenues, Manny had the courage to sign on as a sponsor of the landmark Clear Air, Clean Water, and Endangered Species Acts. He was particularly active on the Indian Affairs subcommittee seeking to improve the circumstances of the Indians in the pueblos and reservations of New Mexico.

And there were areas where junior Republicans could make a difference. When Manny arrived in the Congress, the House was in the grip of a seniority system which had caused inertia for decades. The rule was that the most senior member of a committee would automatically become its chairman. There were three chairmen in their 80s and a number in their 70s. In one case, the chairman was senile, and after gaveling the committee into session on the first day of the new Congress, he would not again be seen. Although the subcommittees would be active, the full committee would not meet again.

So, with George Bush as our leader, we asked Gerry to let us change the rule. Gerry, wary of his own elderly ranking members, appointed a committee with 19 members, six seniors in their 70s, six freshmen or sophomore members and seven in the mid-range. In 1970, we reached an agreement and our caucus voted that, IF we became a majority in the 1970 elections, we would ELECT our chairmen. This caused enough consternation among the Democrats that they adopted the same rule.

But four years would elapse until it happened. In 1974, a host of new Democrats were elected in the aftermath of Watergate, and three of their most venerable chairmen were defeated and reduced to the status of ordinary Members.

When Manny came to the Congress in 1969 there was a House rule that allowed particularly controversial votes to be held by teller count rather than votes of record. This was simply a means to disguise tough votes from folks back home who might object. A Democrat would ask for a teller vote and the Members would line up and pass by tellers who counted the Yeas and Nays. The young Republicans cooperated with rebellious young Democrats in 1970 to force the House to change its rules so that teller counts were no longer allowed and all votes had to be of record.

During Manny's time in Congress, there was tremendous bi-partisan support for new national parks and monuments, wilderness areas, game preserves, and the preservation of habitats for endangered species. In these categories New Mexico has, more than most States, an incredible number of ancient ruins where people had lived on the North American continent for thousands of years. It has its own famous battlefields, such as the one at Glorieta Pass, just east of Santa Fe, where New Mexicans, in 1862, supported by volunteers from Colorado, saved New Mexico for the Union against a Confederate army which had occupied most of the Rio Grande valley in the Civil War.

Manny sponsored bills to establish a private national health protection plan, to reduce taxes on the elderly, regulate waste management, and bills for the protection of the Bandolier wilderness area, Pecos National Monument, Chola

National Forest, and the Manzano and Sandia Mountain wilderness areas.

In the legislative process, Republicans often sought to terminate, or at least limit, federal expenditures.

On one memorable occasion, Manny got the Chairman of his Interior Committee, Mo Udall of Arizona, to cut $1.75 million from a bill appropriating money for various groups of people in the environmental movement, but which included a provision including $2 million for protesters. Mo, a good friend of Manny's and mine, had a handful of proxies from his colleagues, and when Manny offered an amendment in committee to delete the $2 million, Mo quickly defeated it. Then Manny started to offer a whole series of amendments, one at a time for each group of beneficiaries so that each would get only $1 dollar. After Mo had defeated the first three he finally grinned at Manny who was waiting with a whole stack of similar amendments, and inquired "OK, Manny, will you settle for $250,000 for the protesters?" Manny grinned back and said "Fine." The deal was done; $1.75 million was deleted.

I had made a similar compromise with Mo Udall when he was engaged in the monumental effort to put together a fair Alaskan Lands Bill. There were extremely controversial issues as to which lands and areas would be set aside for native Americans and environmental protection, as against development interests. John Dingell, the chairman of our small Fish & Wildlife Conservation Subcommittee who had gotten me to co-author so many environmental bills, had taken me on an eight-day tour of the disputed areas, including the north slope with its oil drilling potential. We had become great friends in pushing through bills like the National Environmental Protection Act in 1969, and in bills to protect Endangered Species habitat, estuarine areas, coastal zones and whales in the early 1970s.

But to enact his landmark but very controversial Alaskan Lands Bill, Mo Udall needed eight votes I controlled which related to a conservationist desire to protection of the annual migration of caribou between U.S. and Canadian lands. Mo came down to my office to spend over an hour with me, discussing what kind of compromise would be acceptable. We finally agreed, and with the eight votes, Mo's bill passed. The importance of the bill was recognized nationally, and some 300 participants from Congress and the various environmental groups were invited to the White House by Jimmy Carter to witness his signature. The President made a brief speech congratulating the Congress, and particularly Mo's leadership. Then Mo made a few typically self-deprecating remarks. His applause was much greater than that given the President, and I remember my own feeling at the time that it was a shame Mo Udall, rather than Carter, hadn't won the Democratic nomination in 1976.

The two examples cited above were ordinary occurrences in the 1970s and 1980s. It was that kind of Congress where friends who respected each other accommodated opposing views by reasoned debate and friendly compromise. The real legislative compromises were generally reached in subcommittee and committee. Because he was respected by his subcommittee and committee chairmen, Manny was able to prevent cutting of funds for Indian schools and later to increase the funds for that purpose.

I should add here a word about House staffs. Perhaps the greatest lesson I learned in 15 years in the House was that women were often more competent than men.

In those days, the House was made up mostly of men,

but a greater number of their offices were run by extremely competent young women. Often, it was their skills and abilities which meant the re-election of their employers.

I had a succession of particularly smart and idealistic young people, both as interns and staffers, but also as Administrative Assistants (AAs). One went on to be the Dean of the UCLA Law School and Provost at Dartmouth. One, Susan Packard, became head of one of the nation's largest philanthropic foundations. One of my best AAs was Celia McFarland from San Mateo County who managed to get me through that terrible summer of 1972, when I was practically banished from the party for my opposition to Nixon. Celia went on to law school, and became the General Counsel to a major national railroad.

In many ways, a congressional office was a wonderful educational place. Advancement could be swift. A woman could start out as a receptionist, advance to being a legislative assistant, and ultimately an AA, in a relatively brief period of time. The key word for their success was "effectiveness".

One example is worth citing. Donna Williams, wife of a young attorney at the SEC, came to work as a receptionist. But she asked for more rewarding work, and when I became the ranking Republican on the Fish & Wildlife Subcommittee, Donna moved over to be subcommittee staff. Before one of Nixon's State of the Union speeches in 1970 or 1971, the White House took a poll and found out that the saving of whales rated fifth in matters of public interest. A White House staffer asked around at the National Fisheries Administration and several Democrat offices and learned that Donna was Washington's acknowledged expert on whales. Thus, two years after she went to work in the House, Donna was asked for, and wrote, two sentences about whales which

Nixon included in his State of the Union speech, so that he could stress his strong interest in saving whales.

Thus, a highly-competent woman staffer could be effective indeed. I'm not sure but that the best possible education for a 17 or 18-year-old idealistic young person is a 3-month internship in a House or Senate office.

But Manny's priority was not in legislation, but in service to his constituents.

Members of Congress were then entitled to have a staff of eleven or twelve. Most new Members had eight or nine staffers in their Washington offices specializing in legislative affairs, with two or three back home. Manny had a different priority. He chose to have a majority of his staff in three local offices, in Albuquerque, Santa Fe, and Las Vegas, and only 4 or 5 in Washington.

One of his first legislative assistants in Washington was Peach Mayer's son, Tom, a gifted writer, who after being educated at Andover and Harvard, chose to go to Viet Nam during the toughest years of the war, in the late 1960's. Tom had studied under the famous Wallace Stegner at Stanford and went to Viet Nam as an accredited reporter to get a first-hand look at the problems our troops were facing. He returned as an anti-war advocate, a position he shared with his parents. His mother had become so disenchanted with the war that she had given Manny Lujan Jr. her support only because she realized that his only hope of election was not to enrage the super patriots who, in 1968, formed the majority of voters in New Mexico.

The patriotism of New Mexicans was legendary. They had furnished more cowboy volunteers for Teddy Roosevelt's Rough Riders of the Spanish American War than any other state. In World War I, New Mexico had more volunteers per capita than any other state. And in Viet Nam, the percentage of infantry casualties was much higher among Hispanic Americans. They were often unable to take advantage of the deferments that were obtainable by college students and men like Dick Cheney, Bill Clinton, and Donald Trump.

In my own experience, the Albuquerque Marine Reserve unit that trained with us at Camp Pendleton for two weeks each summer, with its large number of Hispanic volunteers, always turned in the best performance among the dozens of reserve units. In Korea, some of my best Marines had been of Hispanic ancestry.

Nevertheless, it took New Mexicans a long time before they learned of the deceits of Lyndon Johnson, Robert McNamara and Dean Rusk that led the Congress to approve the Gulf of Tonkin Resolution of 1964, giving the President the right "to meet aggression with aggression in Southeast Asia."

But if no freshman Congressman could hope to work to bring the Viet Nam War to a conclusion, as Manny's friends Peach and Walter Mayer devoutly hoped he would, or seriously change Democrat priorities in legislation, he could certainly see to it that the problems of his constituents with immigration, Social Security, tax matters, veterans and other issues were met. To Manny, his constituents rated the very best help with the bureaucracy that he could provide. The bureaucrats knew who funded their agencies, and a polite but firm call from a congressional staff person could often unsnarl the red tape or other snags which denied constituents fair relief.

In due course, Manny rose to become the Ranking Minority Member on two committees, Interior, and Science and Technology, and thus became a member of the Republican leadership. But for all of his twenty years in the House,

Anwar Sadat, President of Egypt; Tip O'Neill, Speaker of the House; and Manuel Lujan, Congressman.

the Republicans would remain the minority party.

Even so, those twenty years were ones of mutual friendship and respect between many of the Members on both sides of the aisle. Most of us lived in Washington during the week, returning to our Districts perhaps once or twice a month. We and our spouses attended the same dinners, picnics and gatherings. There were annual baseball and basketball games, and once a memorable decathlon between the Republican and Democrats. During Manny's twenty years of service in the House, there was bi-partisan cooperation in the fields of the environment and the attempted revision of the entitlement and immigration laws. Respected Republicans could offer quality amendments from time to time and have them accepted. That way of cooperation has been lost in the House of recent years, to the detriment of the nation.

There were also bi-partisan delegations authorized, during congressional recesses, to visit foreign countries. Both Manny and I took advantage of these opportunities every time we could, spending time in places like China, India, Pakistan, Latin America, Europe, Africa, and the Mideast. These visits provided a necessary education to Americans whose horizons usually began and ended at their own District or State borders. Our decisions increasingly involved familiarity with the customs and politics of foreign nations.

An interesting example occurred in 1982 when President Reagan proposed to sell AWACS reconnaissance planes to Saudi Arabia. Israel and its many supporters in the Congress were outraged. The AWACS would be able to monitor the take offs of Israeli warplanes should they choose to attack Iraq or Egypt.

The issue was a close one. Vice President Bush, accompanied by Egypt's President, Anwar Sadat, came to the House to try to persuade us to approve the sale. The issue was finally decided when Sadat flashed his famous grin, and said to the highly-suspicious Jewish members: "And you know, gentlemen: no Arab will ever be able to operate the AWACS".

And since we Republicans were in the minority, having little power, it wasn't often we were approached with bribes. In the famous Abscam scandal, a number of Democrats took money from the FBI sting, but only one Republican. All went to jail. The same was true when the Korean Evangelist, Father Moon, sent hordes of his young people to lobby in Washington, and a great deal of money was dispensed, nearly all of it to Democrats.

On my Merchant Marine & Fisheries Committee, four of my five Democrat chairmen went to jail during my 15 years in the House, one being convicted in the courthouse in Baltimore which had been named after him. A leading California Democrat, Don Edwards, the Dean of our delegation, once told me that any bill coming out of our committee should go to the Grand Jury instead of the floor.

The Nixon Years: The Southern Strategy

Prior to the 1968 Republican Convention, perhaps the greatest difference between the Republican and Democrat Parties, was that the Republican Party was still the Party of Lincoln, treasuring its policy of improving the civil rights of minorities, protecting the rights of black people, the majority of whom lived in the South. The South, solidly Democrat since the end of Reconstruction after the Civil War, had retained its history of racism, insisting on white supremacy, denying voting rights to black people through devices like the poll tax, and pure simple intimidation of blacks and economic retribution if they tried to vote or break the required racial segregation in buses, trains and lunch counters.

Seeing the South turning away from racial discrimination after the end of World War II, South Carolina Senator Strom Thurmond broke from the Democrat Party in 1948, forming the "Dixiecrat Party." Thurmond won four southern states in the presidential election that year, when Harry Truman won against Republican Governor Tom Dewey of New York.

During the Korean War, Truman terminated racial segregation in the armed services.

Then, following the assassination of Jack Kennedy in 1963, Lyndon Johnson of Texas ascended to the White House. With his unmatched knowledge of the House and Senate, he was able to bludgeon passage of the Civil Rights Acts of 1964 and the Voting Rights Act of 1965, bills which struck a major blow for black people's rights, but were an anathema to Southerners who considered them an insult to the Southern way of life and pursuit of happiness.

By the summer of 1968 it was clear that Governor George Wallace of Mississippi, was going to do very well as a third-party white supremacist in the Southern states, following in Thurmond's footsteps twenty years earlier.

The 1968 Republican Convention

As the Republican Convention approached in Miami in the summer of 1968, there were three major candidates in contention for the 1,149 delegate votes.

Nixon had the lead with somewhat over 500 delegates committed to him for the first ballot, gained chiefly in previous years of attending fund-raising dinners around the country for state and local Republican candidates. It was well-known, however, that a good number of those delegates were not that fond of Nixon personally, and that after the first ballot many would turn to either the liberal Governor Nelson Rockefeller of New York, or more likely, to the bright new conservative star, California Governor Ronald Reagan.

Both Rockefeller and Reagan went to the convention with something in the neighborhood of 225 delegates each. That left perhaps only a little over 100 delegates apparently uncommitted.

Nixon well knew that if he couldn't get the necessary 575 votes on the first ballot, his presidential candidacy was ended, undoubtedly forever.

So what could he do to insure those 575 first ballot votes? He devised a clever, but incredibly indecent policy. He would make a pact with the Devil. He recruited Senator Thurmond to be his spokesman to promise the southern delegates, that if elected, he would REFUSE TO ENFORCE THE 1964 AND 1965 VOTING AND CIVIL RIGHTS ACTS!

I had been in the House only a few months, and was naive about all things politic, but was asked by seven of the more moderate Republican Members if I would join them in going to the Convention to work for Rockefeller. We holed up at one of the main hotels where the delegates were staying. On the first day, Barber Conable, a distinguished older Member from New York, and I were prowling the halls looking for delegates to buttonhole, when we heard a loud voice issuing out from behind the curtains of one of the meeting rooms. We parted the curtains and found ourselves at the back of a long room with perhaps 200 seated delegates, obviously southern by virtue of their boots, Stetsons, etc.

At the far end of the room a small man was thundering. It was Strom Thurmond. His message was loud and clear.

"I know all you southerners want to vote for the true conservative, Ronald Reagan, but if you will stick with Nixon, he has promised he will stop all enforcement of the Voting Rights and Civil Rights Acts."

Barber and I slunk out. We couldn't believe what we were hearing, but it was clear we had little hope to convince any southerners to vote for Rockefeller.

The more people we talked to, the clearer it became that it

would not be our candidate that would win if Nixon failed to win on the first ballot. There was clear preference for Reagan.

Finally, the balloting commenced in alphabetical order. It wasn't until the delegates from Washington voted, that Nixon reached the necessary 575 votes. He ended up with 591 votes, sixteen over what he needed. With the assassination of Bobby Kennedy following his euphoric primary victory in California, Nixon was elected President.

For the first time in history, a President had been elected despite a promise that he would not faithfully execute the laws of the United States as the oath he would shortly take required.

Nixon's perfidy didn't affect the Congress much. But it did infect his Administration. My former law partner, Lewis Butler, was acting as the No. 1 Assistant Secretary at HEW, when the White House demanded that he fire a young Republican lawyer, Leon Panetta, then in charge of enforcing the school desecration policies in southern states as ordered by the Supreme Court in the Brown vs. Board of Education decision. The reason for the order was stated in no uncertain terms; "Doesn't he know the President has promised that he wouldn't enforce the Civil Rights Acts?"

Lewis and his superiors, Bob Finch and Jack Veneman refused and threatened to resign, and the White House backed down. But Panetta got the word. He resigned, returned to California, changed to the Democrat Party and in 1976 ousted a long-time Republican from the House. Leon went on to become a good friend of both Manny and me, became Chairman of the important Budget Committee, and with that expertise, became President Clinton's Chief of Staff, and in the late 1990s achieved the first and last balanced budget in the past several decades.

Nixon's resumption of the heavy bombing of Southeast Asia at Christmastime, 1972, caused Lew Butler to quietly resign, sending a short letter to Nixon, stating that he and other Americans would feel the shame and sorrow of the bombing for the rest of their lives. He quietly left Washington to return to California to work in the fields of environmental protection and limitation of nuclear proliferation.

Nixon was even less successful in seeking to appoint Supreme Court justices to try and eviscerate the Civil Rights and Voting Rights Acts. He nominated two reputable southerner judges, Clement Haynesworth and G. Harold Carswell, but the Senate rejected both on the grounds of their obvious racism.

Carswell had once said:

"I yield to no man as a fellow candidate, or as a fellow citizen, in the firm vigorous belief in the principle of white supremacy."

Nixon's Second Term

Although Nixon was re-elected overwhelmingly in 1972, his problems increased enormously. They were not easy years for Republicans in the Congress. The publication of the Pentagon Papers in June, 1971, and the Watergate burglary investigation drew increasing public attention and rage, not lessened when it turned out that Vice President Agnew was alleged to have taken over $300,000 in bribes and payoffs as Governor of Maryland, with money still coming in to him as Vice President. Senator Ervin's Committee and the writings of Woodward and Bernstein of the Washington Post continued to bring unsavory matters at the White House to public attention, and finally Attorney General Elliot Richardson was able to force Agnew to resign in turn for being allowed to plead guilty to a single count of tax evasion.

With the House Judiciary Committee, including four staunch Republicans voting to impeach Nixon, he finally resigned in disgrace in early August, 1974.

The nation sighed with relief, as did Congressional Republicans, and we voted that Gerry Ford become our next Vice President under the recently-enacted Constitutional Amendment.

As the transcripts of the Nixon tapes have become publicly available, I'm afraid that the most accurate words to describe Nixon were those of Senator Bob Dole of Kansas:

"Ford, See No Evil; Reagan: Hear No Evil; Nixon: EVIL"

The Short Presidency of Gerry Ford

Manny, like me and most of his colleagues, had come to revere Gerry Ford as perhaps the most humane and decent political figure in Washington. He and I particularly believed, from daily association with Gerry, that he would never have agreed to pardon Nixon if Nixon named him to be Vice-President. He just wasn't that kind of man. He had a deep compassion, but was not a man to make deals like trading an appointment as Vice President for a pardon of Nixon.

We all remember the euphoria that swept the nation when the long years of Watergate ended with Nixon's resignation and Ford's being sworn in as President. But then the Congress recessed, and, with none of us around to suggest otherwise, Ford's worries of a continuation of the dark days that had preceded him by the further prosecution of Nixon took hold and he pardoned his disgraced predecessor.

Public perception of that pardon, however, was uniformly

adverse. Suspicion was widespread that Ford had made a deal with Nixon; if appointed Vice President he would pardon Nixon. That perception probably cost Ford the election in 1976, with Reagan publicly remaining aloof, hoping to become President himself, as he was finally able to do in 1980. Manny Lujan Jr. had become a close friend of Ford, and he and I campaigned for him in 1976, both in the primary against Reagan and in the general against Jimmy Carter.

The cooperation and mutual respect between Republicans and Democrats in Congress would last until the accession to power of Newt Gingrich as Speaker in 1995. The years between 1968 and 1988 would see three Republican Presidents, Nixon, Ford, and Reagan, all working with a Democrat majority in the House. Those years marked the passage of numerous new environmental protection laws and the creation of a large number of new National Parks, wildlife refuges and wilderness areas. But most of all they marked courtesy, comity, and considerable congeniality and respect amongst the Members of the House.

But all this ended when Newt Gingrich became Speaker. There would be two Speakers to follow of questionable morality and numerous scandals, with Denny Hastert ultimately going to jail for covering up the molestation of young men. While John Boehner and Paul Ryan are clearly honorable men, they have had enormous difficulty in obtaining the effective passage of laws during their terms in office. It is fair to say that Congress has been completely immobilized for the past eight years by the contentious hostility of Republicans towards their Democrat colleagues which makes difficult the necessary cooperation which could lead to legislation not subject to veto by the Democrat President.

Parts of my former District are now occupied by three superb women: Anna Eshoo, Jackie Speier, and Zoe Lofgren, all three Democrats. It is the same with Manny's old district – now two districts, both represented by relatives of his, and both Democrat. Neither Michelle Lujan Grisham of Albuquerque and Ray Luján representing Santa Fe, receive the common courtesy and friendly respect of their Republican colleagues that Manny and I had received from the Democrats of our day.

The lack of courtesy and respect between the parties is a tragedy. The low public opinion of Congress reflects that tragedy only too greatly. The rancor in Congress has also caused me to rethink my youthful feelings of male superiority. The personages of First Ladies, Laura Bush, and Michelle Obama, and most of the Congresswomen I know, seem far more thoughtful and substantive, far less militant and confrontational than has been the dialogue between the male leaders of both parties in recent years.

Manny's first election, in 1968, had been followed by his re-election nine times, usually by hefty margins, though the District remained one with a Democrat majority. On only one occasion did he have a close call, that being in 1980, when he was considerably outspent by another Hispanic-American, Bill Richardson.

The 1980 close call taught Manny that he should raise more money to fend off challengers, and in the process he amassed a substantial sum. In 1981, he used some of the funds he hadn't used for his re-election to set up The First Congressional District Scholarship Fund to award scholarships to deserving high school graduates who aspired to go on to New Mexico colleges. He raised money through boxing, wrestling, and tennis matches, and all sorts of entertaining events. In 1988, he donated $125,000 of his unused campaign money to the Fund. That was money he could have spent on himself and his family.

Scholarships of $500 per year were awarded for four years of college. As of this writing in late 2016, the Fund has contributed 27 scholarships each year for a total of 108 to six New Mexican colleges. The Fund is now administered by the Albuquerque Community Foundation, in order to avoid political interference.

Sadly, neither Manny's mother or father lived to see him carry on the legacy of their own contributions to the education of the forgotten people of Northern New Mexico, or the high honor of his appointment by President George H. W. Bush to serve as Secretary of the Interior for the nation. They would have been proud indeed.

On January 4, 1988, after being re-elected by an overwhelming margin for his 10th term in Congress, Manny announced that he would retire at the end of his term. He simply stated: "The basic reason is that I see so many of my colleagues stay too long. After 20 years it is time to come home."

Manny had had enough of Washington, its pomp, fancy dinners and arrogant self-importance. He was fairly unique in this respect. A huge majority of his colleagues, ("Few die and none retire") had chosen upon defeat or retirement to stay within the Beltway and earn far more than their congressional salaries as lobbyists or heads of national organizations dealing with the issues they had focused on in the Congress.

Not so for Manny. A year later he would think long and hard before he finally accepted the request of his friend, George H.W. Bush, that he serve as President Bush's Secretary of the Interior.

Chapter 6

The Congressman Casts Two Key Votes Against the Bombing 1972 and 1973

There were probably a lot of votes that Manuel Lujan may have not wanted to cast in his 20 years in Congress. One, in particular, however, drew national attention. It was cast on television before an audience of millions.

It happened in August, 1972, and it was the direct result of the scheming and plotting of Manny's great friend and supporter, Peach Mayer.

No one should ever forget a fact learned only late in life by most American men. One very smart and beautiful woman can do almost anything if she puts her mind to it.

In early 1972, Peach learned from the newspapers that an obscure, and apparently deranged Korean war vet with PTSD was challenging Nixon and his Viet Nam War policies in the Republican primary in New Hampshire. The misguided man apparently had the delusion that he could replicate what Senator Eugene McCarthy had done in the 1968 Democrat primary...getting 40% of the vote, and leading to LBJ's announcement that he wouldn't run for the Presidency again. This misguided man was me.

But shortly before the New Hampshire primary, Nixon pulled a masterstroke, perhaps the finest act of his presidential years. HE WENT TO CHINA. For weeks the television was blanketed with pictures of the Great Wall, smiling Chinese, and panda bears. There would be no need to debate paltry matters like the secret heavy bombing in Southeast Asia.

I wound up on March 7, 1972, with only 19.9% of the New Hampshire Republican Presidential Primary vote, and promptly dropped out of the race in despair, returning to face a disillusioned Republican constituency in my own Congressional district in California, which was still highly enamored of Nixon. I was not expected to win my own House primary race in June.

But here entered again that dedicated anti-war advocate, Manny Lujan's friend and benefactor, the wily New Mexican

The Albuquerque Tribune, June 5, 1972.

Note that this ad was paid for by Peach Mayer.

political operator, Peach Mayer. The Grande Dame of New Mexico Republicanism devised a plot to get at least one vote at the Republican National Convention against the bombing.

Peach knew that New Mexico's voting law allowed proportionate assignment of its 14 Republican delegates to the Republican National Convention. She promptly called my congressional office and got consent to enter my name on the New Mexican primary ballot for the Presidency.

When I agreed, she dragged along her reluctant son, Tom, to see an old friend next door, Betty Fiorina, the Democrat Secretary of State. The deadline for filing for presidential candidates had long since passed. Peach, however, with her usual charm, was able to persuade her friend to make an exception and put my name on the June ballot. No doubt, Ms. Fiorina perceived there might be an advantage to Democrats by causing some chaos in the Republican primary. But who would know or even care?

Peach and Tom split the $150 filing fee, paying $75 each.

I had promised I would take advantage of Tom's offer to fly me in Tom's ancient yellow stagger-wing biplane up and down the Rio Grande, but alas, had to stay in California to try to survive my own congressional primary in June, a considerable long shot in view of the general outrage felt by my Republican constituents.

But there were rebels in the colleges of New Mexico, especially down in Socorro at New Mexico State University where they were led by a prankster, Bill Diven. The fun of attacking the establishment was too good an opportunity to miss. Despite their distaste for Nixon, many of them, newly enfranchised, registered as Republican solely to express a vote against the war. There was also a cadre of older, moderate Republicans opposed to the war. The result was unexpected.

A candidate most New Mexicans never heard of, and who had never campaigned in New Mexico, got nearly 7% of the vote, thereby becoming entitled by law to one of New Mexico's 14 delegates to the Republican National Convention.

Peach led her unorthodox candidate down to the State convention in Albuquerque with my agreement that her son, Tom, would be named as my delegate, entitled to put my name in nomination at the upcoming national Republican convention in Miami.

The New Mexico State convention was held in a vast hall with several hundred Republicans eyeing Peach's candidate with some suspicion. The Chairman inquired if I would agree to make the vote unanimous for Nixon if Nixon won on the first ballot. I had observed the results of bombing of civilian villages in the Korean War in my youth, and was fully aware of the incredible bombing campaign being run

in Viet Nam, Laos, and Cambodia by huge B-52s dropping strings of 2,000 pound bombs. I replied simply: "Only if he stops the bombing."

There were boos and hisses, and the Chairman received unanimous approval to a motion that the dissenting one's delegate would be decided by the Convention. Congressman Lujan was given the unenviable task of casting that outrageous vote, instead of Peach's son, at the National Convention.

Thus it was that Tom Mayer and I went to Miami, registering in one of the long line of skyscraper hotels. Tom presented his credentials to the credential committee, and was treated with scorn and told to go away. Tom commented to a few uncaring reporters that he thought Leon Trotsky might have gotten a fairer hearing at Nuremberg than he had gotten.

It was learned that Nixon's No. 2 assistant, John

Students at Peace Rally, New Mexico State College, June 1972

The leaders of 2,000+ Viet Nam vets outside the Fountainbleau Hotel in August, 1972, demanding a meeting with President Nixon.

Ehrlichman, had engineered a rule that only if a candidate had 25 delegates would he or any of his delegates even be allowed on the floor of the convention. Ehrlichman later revealed to Peach on her 80th birthday in 1985 that there had been concerns raised by Nixon's advisors about the danger of a vitriolic speech by Tom Mayer, in nominating his candidate and excoriating Nixon's bombing campaign. He told her that they had listened into (wiretapped) the telephone conversations between me and my Administrative Assistant, Celia McFarland, and learned that Tom's speech would be a vitriolic attack on Nixon's bombing policy. "Peach, we couldn't allow that," Ehrlichman told her. Peach, who would die shortly thereafter, simply replied, "I thought so."

On a steamy summer day, a straggly group of some 2,000 or more anti-war veterans marched to the Fountainbleu Hotel, the Nixon headquarters, to demand an audience with Nixon himself. They were led by Ron Kovics and four other amputees in wheel chairs, but were barred from the hotel by a long line of Miami police, elbow to elbow, with helmet visors, shields and billy clubs. The vets were lean and hungry in faded combat fatigues, and they were both angry and dedicated. The officers, many with bellies hanging over their belts, were understandably reluctant to try to take on the vets.

It was a terribly hot day, hot enough that the asphalt in the street was melting. There was real danger of violence and bloodshed.

And here it was that Tom Mayer, a veteran of two tours in Viet Nam as a reporter, did a memorable and courageous thing. He went into the hotel and, after a contentious debate with the manager, paid with his own money for a wooden case holding 24 bottles of warm Coca Cola, accompanying me as we shouldered through the police line and delivered the cokes to the thirsty leaders of the march. I flashed my congressional credentials, and the Major in charge let me and Tom through to talk with the leaders in their wheelchairs.

There was obvious consternation in the line of police. Those coke bottles looked like very handy weapons if thrown like grenades, a skill the police knew many of the veterans had mastered in Viet Nam. The Major in command could see that no great benefit would result if the vets chose to storm his line. His men obviously agreed with him. They had no desire to take on veterans who had risked their lives for the nation.

Negotiations were held, and a compromise was reached. The Major finally agreed that three of the vet leaders in wheel chairs would be allowed into the hotel to meet with the President's representatives.

The next compromise was reached in the hotel lobby. The three, with only two good legs between them, one double amputee and two single amputees, would not meet with a high member of Nixon's entourage, but would be allowed a place high in the convention audience for the final voting.

The convention affair was a coronation, not an orderly affair. My sorrows were somewhat ameliorated by being invited to dinner by Walter Cronkite, beloved CBS news anchorman, with the editor of the Miami paper. I missed the long Convention voting process and the thunderous applause of "FOUR MORE YEARS, FOUR MORE YEARS," from the assembled Republican Party faithful.

As the voting by states proceeded and it became New Mexico's turn, Manuel Lujan Jr. rose to his feet and proudly shouted:

'The sovereign state of New Mexico casts 13 votes for that great American, Richard Nixon, and..." (sotto voce, behind his hand) "one vote for Paul McCloskey."

There were scattered boos and hisses. But the three Viet Nam vets in their wheel chairs saw and seized their moment. As the TV cameras played over the enthusiastic audience, and the lights reached them, they reached under their seats and held up three brown cardboard box panels with the words "STOP THE BOMBING."

They were immediately overwhelmed and obscured by young women in red, white and blue miniskirts, and wheeled ignominiously out the door.

But this bit of whimsy was seen nationwide, inspiring cartoons, one of which was entitled: "Spectre at the Feast," by John Fischetti, portraying the grim reaper holding up one bony finger, "1,347 to 1… One Vote Against the Bombing."

The famous cartoonist, Garry Trudeau, ran a panel depicting the mother of his cartoon character, Zonker, as the solo delegate against Nixon.

That vote might well have been characterized as not that of Manuel Lujan, Jr., but really that of New Mexico's beloved Republican leader, the Grande Dame of Santa Fe, Peach Mayer.

Assistant Secretary of HEW Lewis Butler resigned in December, 1972, citing the renewed bombing of Southeast Asia as so repugnant to his conscience as to require his resignation.

Manny's embarrassment and discomfiture at his State's lack of unanimity for the President lasted less than a year.

On June 25, 1973, the House of Representatives voted to prevent Nixon from ever again resuming bombing in Southeast Asia after August 15th. The last words in the floor debate were those of Minority Leader Gerry Ford, stating that he had just talked to Nixon in San Clemente and that if a pending amendment were defeated, Nixon promised to never again resume the bombing in Southeast Asia. The amendment was defeated on a 204 to 204 tie vote. Manny had voted to end the bombing.

Nixon gained the right to bomb for seven more weeks, but in return he had committed to never again bomb after August 15, 1973.

When Nixon sought in November to renege on his promise and restart the bombing, the General Counsel for the Defense Department, William Howard Taft IV, ruled that Ford's words in the recorded debate on the House floor, and the House vote, prevented the President, by law, from taking such action unless Congress changed the law. Congress never did. It turned out that the United States' inability to resume bombing in April, 1975, forced the defeat of the South Vietnamese and the ignominious flight from Saigon. U.S. bombing had stopped a similar invasion in 1972.

The first lady of New Mexican Republicanism had scored

again. The man she had supported in 1967, had made the key vote six years later that finally and forever ended U.S. bombing in Southeast Asia.

Then, in July, 1974, the House Judiciary Committee, in a bi-partisan vote, with staunch Republicans like Bill Cohen, Tom Railsback, Caldwell Butler, and Hamilton Fish III voting aye, voted to impeach Nixon.

Manny Lujan's great American resigned in disgrace. To many college students back in New Mexico and across the nation, Manny had become a national hero.

Being sworn in by Justice Scalia, 1989

Chapter 7
The Secretary of the Interior

In early 1989, Manny Lujan was sworn in by the President and Supreme Court Justice Scalia as Secretary of the Interior of the United States. He had had no problem with Senate confirmation. New Mexico's two Senators, Republican Pete Domenici and Democrat Jeff Bingaman, spoke proudly and favorably of him when introducing him to their Senate colleagues.

Manny entered his high responsibilities in awe of the perks of office – car and driver, Secret Service protection and all the perquisites of that high office. He became accustomed to them, but never came to believe they were necessary to his peace and well-being. He remained a humble and quiet person, but he enjoyed applying his business skills to the management of his huge department.

Realizing that there could be a conflict with his thriving insurance business in Albuquerque, he sold his half interest. There had been previous insurance operators who had gone into federal and state offices, using the power of those offices to grant favors to their business clientele.

The offices of the Secretary of the Interior are in a huge, high-ceilinged, ancient building on C Street, close to the modern eight story edifice of the Secretary of State.

Many think that the building's most valuable asset is its own full-size basketball court deep in its bowels. It contains offices for a wide variety of its agencies, the Bureau of Indian Affairs, National Park Service, Fish and Wildlife Conservation, the Bureau of Land Management and countless others, all teeming with hard-working bureaucrats working towards retirement with the hope that no untoward event or scandal will erupt to interfere with the substantial retirement funds that Congress has been careful to create for them and the Congresspersons as well. The denizens of that structure, like all career bureaucrats in all of the agencies, are accustomed to look with some suspicion on new Secretaries, appointed by reason of their friendship with the most recently-elected President. The long-time experienced professionals know that it is only a matter of time before the zealous newcomers will probably be replaced in the next Administration. But Manny had been dealing with the Department of the Interior for many years. He took a careful look at its annual budget, and for the second year of his term, successfully recommended a $400 million budget cut.

Prior to Manny's taking office, the prior Secretaries of the Interior, James Watt in particular, under President Reagan, had not been particular friends of environmental protection. They reflected one of Reagan's casual comments: "If you've seen one redwood, you've seen them all."

But Manny, in his 20 years in the House, had joined in sponsoring seven landmark environmental bills. He had been serving on the Interior Committee's Energy and Conservation Committee and was accustomed to fair balancing of energy and environmental interests. He took over the Department with strong views of what he would like to do to correct the Department's administration. There was more than one national conservation group that feared he would be unduly anti-environment in his decisions. He proved them dead wrong.

He promised to do his best to reconcile the strong arguments for energy development with the concerns of the environmental community. And he did.

He announced that he felt his primary duty was as a Trustee... that his guiding principle would be "to turn over to my successor the resources entrusted to me in better condition than when I received them."

He made it a point to visit each of the National Parks and National Monuments and Battlefields and most of the historic and wildlife preserves under his jurisdiction.

Some of his accomplishments:

He immediately banned the use of non-biodegradable or non-recyclable products at the Department's cafeteria and urged all of the National Parks to regulate biodegradable items and their disposal.

He emphasized his dedication to a national policy balancing economic resource development and environmental protection to insure quality of life.

He helped implement President Bush's "no net loss

The President and his Secretary of the Interior and Mrs. Lujan, 1989-1993

of wetlands" goal through actions to enlarge Everglades National Park in Florida, and by supporting passage of the North American Wetlands Conservation Act. The wetlands of his native state of New Mexico were few indeed, but he supported extensive wetlands preservation areas along the Rio Grande for the endangered sandhill crane and other species.

He was good to my home state of California. He proposed a plan to repair the environmental damage to the Kesterson Reservoir, tripling the useful wetlands acreage. He pursued an agreement to force a foreign company to better the management of the concessions at Yosemite National Park. There had been a scandal when he was in Congress over the attempt of a private movie company to desecrate the cliffs of

Yosemite Valley by painting its natural rocks with gray paint to make them stand out more in movie scenes.

He listed the Mojave Desert population of the desert tortoise as an endangered species, thereby saving thousands of square miles from off-road vehicle erosion and habitat destruction.

He reclassified the status of wild chimpanzees from "threatened" to "endangered".

He expanded the Recovery Implementation Program for endangered fish species in the Upper Colorado River Basin.

He established education as the primary goal of the Bureau of Indian Affairs, something that would have brought special joy to his father's heart. He developed a stronger policy to protect sacred objects and human remains on federal lands. He ordered steps to reduce Indian child abuse and neglect.

He launched "Legacy 99," a program to put $1 billion into needed repairs to National Park structures by 1999.

The Manuel Lujan Sr. Building in Santa Fe

Manny's official portrait – hung in the Department of the Interior.

He improved the Department's efforts to hire qualified women and minorities.

He established an Interior Council on Global Climate Change to encourage the Department's strong support in such scientific research. (Note here where today's House and Senate Republican leaders are on this issue… continuing to

Manuel Jr. and Jean at Ellis Island.

contend that man's contribution to global warming is a hoax).

He caused the refurbishment of Ellis Island, the place of entry of so many immigrants to America.

He enraged the west coast timber companies by directing preservation efforts to protect the endangered Spotted Owl.

He established the American Battlefield Protection Program to save historic battlefields for future generations and established a private sector foundation to raise the necessary funds for protecting those battlefields from encroaching commercial and housing development.

He personally participated in monitoring the cleanup of the Exxon Valdez tanker disaster in Alaskan waters.

He led the effort to ban the importation of African elephant ivory.

But Manny had three achievements of which he was

especially proud.

Approached by two of Washington's most prominent personages, one a leading former Democrat national chairman, and the other a prominent Republican Senator, with a request that he approve the turnover of Yosemite to a Japanese corporation, he politely told them to go to hell. He took the position that no Japanese company should operate an American National Park, and negotiated a deal whereby the Japanese would terminate their operation in three years and turn over all of the buildings in the park to the National Park Service. They went over his head to the President, but George H. W. Bush said the matter was up to Manny and sustained his decision.

In another monumental decision, he upped the 2% fee paid by the concessionaires in National Parks to 22.5%, thereby earning an additional $100 million per year to use in the rehabilitation of aging Park structures.

And he was particularly proud of arranging a swap of government lands which added millions of acres to the Everglades National Park in Florida.

But perhaps most importantly of all, he left his cavernous office in January, 1993, after four years without a breath of scandal having touched his administration. During his tenure he had resolutely declined any proffers of advantage to him if he granted favors to the wealthy and powerful.

He returned to Albuquerque to help raise his grandchildren, he and Jean adopting Noah, one of their great grandchildren whom he drove to school for years. He had achieved his primary objective. He was leaving the special places of his country in better condition than when he assumed their trusteeship four years before.

For the past 23 years, he has engaged in a series of

public and private charities, church and other community programs, serving on various boards for local enterprises, including a construction company headquartered at the Laguna Pueblo. There are several buildings named after him, but the major civic building in Santa Fe bears, in huge letters, "The Manuel Lujan Sr. Building." The Lujans, father and son, thus established a whole new ethic of honesty in Republican politics.

This is a special man, at 88, deserving to be honored like his father for major contributions in public service to his state and country.

Hopefully the Manuel Lujan standard will be that to which current and future New Mexican politicians of both parties will be held, and by which they should be judged.

Wrestling an alligator in the Everglades

Reflections

As I read over the preceding chapters, I am reminded of how many values and circumstances have changed since Manny Lujan and I met in Washington in 1969. The Republican Party of today is not the party we knew in the days of Gerry Ford and George H.W. Bush. I can see no benefit from being nostalgic about those days before Newt Gingrich, 9/11, and the wars in Iraq and Afghanistan which changed the role of Congress so much.

Where we wrestled with the War Powers Act in the 1970's, the modern evolution of weaponry has made it almost a moot point over whether Congress has the sole power to authorize war as the Constitution originally intended. The burgeoning national debt, defense budget, a free press versus the national security, dealing not just with nation-states but with men and women of determined religious beliefs in the Muslim world, willing to die for their perceived religion as were the Japanese kamikaze pilots for their guiding Shinto philosophy... these are grave issues that the Congresses prior to the 1970's and 1980's never had to address.

But there is no reason that good people of widely-differing views can't sit down together and, with courtesy and respect, work out reasonable solutions for the entitlement programs, immigration, a balanced budget and a host of other problems which cry out for compromise.

It has to be asked whether a government such as ours can EVER bring itself to tax our citizens for the tremendous costs of our wars and defense budgets.

But if the issues are more complex, there is one thing I believe the people of the United States would like to see again, that being a courteous relationship between the leaders and followers in both parties.

I occasionally call to mind the famous words of Ben Franklin on the last day of the Constitutional Convention of 1787. The draft Constitution had been carved out in the stifling heat of a Philadelphia summer with the windows blocked so that the public would not hear the long and contentious debates.

From Madison's Journal:

"Mr. President: (George Washington presiding)

I confess that there are several parts of this Constitution which I do not at present approve, but I am not sure I shall never approve them. For having lived long, I have experienced many instances of being obliged by better information or fuller consideration, to change my opinions, even on important subjects which I once thought right, but found to be otherwise. It is, therefore, that the older I grow the more apt I am to doubt my own judgment, and to pay more respect to the opinions of others."

Franklin, the oldest of the delegates, then went on to urge unanimous approval of the Constitution "because we are not likely to get a better one."

Since being elected to Congress, I have had to change my opinions on many things, as Manny Lujan changed his opinion on the bombing in Viet Nam. But neither he nor I have changed our views on one point, that those privileged to serve in the House of Representatives should treat each other with courtesy and respect.

In the words of George H.W. Bush, both the Nation and the Congress could well be "kinder and gentler."

Acknowledgments

There are a lot of people I need to thank for putting this small book together.

My wife, Helen, comes first. She was 15 and I was 41 when we first met in 1968, with her parents bringing her home to Woodside, California, after 11 years in Europe where her father worked at ambassadorial level for NATO in Paris. We became the best of friends, and first visited New Mexico together in 1978. We were married in 1982. She is smarter than me, and has also been my long-time editor and critic. Her passion to save all furred and feathered creatures and their habitats, and our shared love for the western landscape and wilderness has been perhaps the motivating feature of our past 37 years of living together. We have backpacked and traveled extensively in the High Sierra for years. Without her skill in untangling the mysteries of modern computer use, these thoughts would never have come to print. She has insisted that we support the causes of American Indians, such as the stand of Sioux at Standing Rock, ND, against the Dakota Access Pipeline, and the Apaches in Arizona in trying to protect their historic lands from contemporary treaty violations promoted by powerful politicians for the benefit of multi-national resource interests. More than most she has insisted on sharing the actions and passions of her time. She has come to love and respect Manny Lujan and the wonders and history of his native state as much as I do.

Second, I owe a debt of gratitude to Manny's niece and the author of *"Children of the Pajarito Plateau,"* Kathryn Cordova of Taos. Her books about New Mexicans and the Lujans have been great guides to a newcomer from California.

Third, Tom Mayer of Española, who hung through those tortuous days of the 1972 Republican Convention with me. Tom has provided much of the information about the parents, both his and Manny's, who did so much to prepare Manny for his service in Washington. Then there is Manny's wife, Jean, whose love and support have clearly given Manny much of his strength.

There are the wonderfully helpful people of the Santa Fe Public Library who spent hours directing me to source materials.

I want also to thank my senior partner, Joe Cotchett, and his partners at Cotchett, Pitre and McCarthy for giving me a base for the past eight years as counsel to a superb, small-town, justice-seeking law firm, while yet letting me have the time to research and write essays like this one.

Finally, great credit is due that ace book designer of Madrid, New Mexico, Barbara Fail, who somehow managed to get everything together.

In retrospect I'm not sure I've done full justice to what I wanted to portray... the story of a rare, thoughtful, and honest public servant, with a little history about the State he has represented so well. Ideally, I suppose I had hoped to describe a model for other Members of Congress to seek to emulate in the future. There are two of his relatives who bear the Lujan name now serving in Congress, and while both are Democrats, I believe they are living up to the legacy of both Manuel Lujans, Sr. and Jr., as well as the long line of Hispanic-Indian Lujans who stood up to the rigors of this harsh but beautiful landscape starting back in 1598.

Afterword

In closing, the words of "America The Beautiful" are worth thinking about.

O beautiful for spacious skies, for amber waves of grain,
For purple mountain majesties, above the fruited plain!
America! America! God shed His grace on thee
And crown thy good with brotherhood
From sea to shining sea!

It's the word "brotherhood" that finally hit me while trying to understand what was unique about Manny Lujan. It was the sense of brotherhood he contributed to the lives of those in Washington, trying to craft laws that work, with Gerry Ford and George Bush the Elder and the many dedicated people in Congress who shared that Constitutionally-imposed and ever-changing task, of enacting appropriate laws that worked for all the people, not just the few.

Perhaps most of all it is the sense of kinship with the land and creatures that Terry Tempest Williams so well describes in her books… that sense of deep connection with the lands in his own state of New Mexico and the National Parks and places like Gettysburg and Antietam and the Little Big Horn and Glorietta Pass and the men and women who fought and died on both sides in those places, believing in the causes for which they fought. We can enjoy the incredible blue skies, sunsets, and towering cloud formations of New Mexico in relative comfort, but there is always the reminder of the bones of the women, children, and men buried beneath our feet, the Indians, and the Spanish settlers, and those 400 years of privation and hunger that preceded our present generation with our air-conditioned cars and homes.

Nixon's "southern strategy" has been successful, beyond his fondest expectations. In the 2016 election only two weeks ago, all of the former Confederate states of the "Solid South," save Virginia, voted Republican. New Mexico did not. The Republicans, riding a populist wave of antagonism to Washington D.C. and a candidate linked to the political and financial elite. Although they did not win a majority vote, they are now in command at the White House, Senate and House, and with the right to make the next Supreme Court appointment, now have the absolute power to govern. We can hope that they will not fall to that ancient rule of politics that "Power Corrupts; Absolute Power Corrupts Absolutely." There is much to clean up in Washington.

The hope of Helen and me is that the next Congress will convene in a new spirit of brotherhood, and now sisterhood ... that individual Members from the 50 states will fight and argue hard for their beliefs, but then sit down in subcommittee, committee, and finally on the House floor, working with respect and courtesy for each other, and seeking reasonable compromises in legislation. A naive hope? Perhaps, but why not try?

If the Members of the next Congress do this, in the spirit and courteous manner of the 24 years of public service of Manny Lujan, the country will be well served.

Pete McCloskey
Madrid, New Mexico,
Thanksgiving Day, 2016
P.O. Box 158
Cerrillos, New Mexico, 87010
email: rumseyfarm@aol.com

About the Author

By Helen Hooper McCloskey, the author's friend and spouse of 30+ years. Written as an editor's prerogative and over the author's objections.

Pete, a small-town trial lawyer, graduated from Stanford Law School in 1953, the year I was born. He served as a Deputy District Attorney in Alameda County until 1955. He founded the firm of McCloskey & Wilson in 1958, in Palo Alto, California, which subsequently evolved into the 600+ member firm of Wilson, Sonsini, Goodrich & Rosati. He was President of the Palo Alto Bar Association in 1960, the Conference of Barristers of the State Bar in 1961, and served as a Trustee of the Santa Clara Bar Association from 1964 through 1967. He has taught political science, legal ethics and constitutional law at Stanford and Santa Clara Universities, and lectured at the Army War College of Carlisle, Pennsylvania, and the Marine Corps Staff College at Quantico, Virginia.

Pete received the Navy Cross, Silver Star and two Purple Hearts for his courage and wounds received in combat, as a Marine rifle platoon leader in the Korean War. He was elected to the U.S. House of Representatives in 1967, and re-elected seven times, representing the San Francisco Peninsula area, including Silicon Valley. Pete served, with Senator Gaylord Nelson, as the co-Chairman of the first Earth Day in 1970, and ran for the Republican nomination for the Presidency in 1972, challenging President Nixon's Viet Nam War policy.

He challenged Israel's use of cluster bombs in Lebanon, and spoke out against Israel's illegal settlements, in the occupied West Bank and Palestinian territories in violation of international law. He made the first speech on the House floor advocating that the House consider impeachment proceedings against Nixon on June 6, 1973, on the grounds of obstruction of justice. This was the first Article of Impeachment adopted by the House Judiciary Committee a year later. He was a co-author of the Endangered Species Act and served six years as Congressional Delegate to the International Whaling Conference, and as Congressional Advisor to the Law of the Sea Treaty Delegation under Chairmen John Stevenson and Elliot Richardson. He was appointed by President George H.W. Bush to the U.S. Commission on National and Community Service in 1990, confirmed by the Senate and elected as its first Chairman for three years. In 2006, Pete came out of retirement to challenge Congressman Richard Pombo in the Republican primary in California's 11th Congressional District, because of Pombo's efforts, as Chairman of the House Resources Committee, to eviscerate the Endangered Species Act. He lost, but the effort cost Pombo his seat. His family having been Republicans in California since 1859, Pete, in 2007, disgusted with the acceptance of torture and violations of International Law by the Bush Administration, became a Democrat. He was particularly incensed by the legal opinions of Alberto Gonzales, John Yoo, and David Addington, who felt the President was entitled to authorize the torture of enemy captives in violation of the Geneva Convention.

ABOUT THE AUTHOR

He has written four books: *The U.S. Constitution* (BRL, 1961); *Truth and Untruth – Political Deceit in America* (Simon and Schuster, 1971); *The Taking of Hill 610* (Eaglet Books, 1992); and *A Year in a Marine Rifle Company – Korea, 1950-51* (Eaglet Books, 2013).

CPSIA information can be obtained
at www.ICGtesting.com
Printed in the USA
FSOW04n0225151216
28592FS